BLOOD & HATE

BLOOD &

HATE

DAVE WEDGE

THE UNTOLD STORY OF MARVELOUS MARVIN HAGLER'S BATTLE FOR GLORY

HAMILCAR
PUBLICATIONS
BOSTON

Copyright © 2025 Dave Wedge

All rights reserved. No part of this book may be reproduced in any form or by any means, electronic or mechanical, including photocopying, recording, or by any information storage and retrieval system without permission in writing from the publisher.

Paperback ISBN: 978-1-949590-84-5

Hardcover ISBN: 978-1-949590-83-8

hamilcarpubs.com

Aut viam inveniam aut faciam

This book is dedicated to the people of Brockton—the City of Champions—and my parents, Arlene and Roger, for raising me in such a proud city. And thanks Dad, for taking me to my first pro boxing match at Boston Garden where I watched Marvelous Marvin Hagler beat up Vito "The Mosquito" Antuofermo, making me a boxing fan for life.

CONTENTS

CHAPTER 1
NEWARK . . . 1

CHAPTER 2
SUMMER OF '67 . . . 9

CHAPTER 3
BROCKTON . . . 19

CHAPTER 4
GOODY AND ROCKY . . . 23

CHAPTER 5
ROCKY'S RISE . . . 29

CHAPTER 6
ROCKY, THE MOB, AND A FATEFUL FLIGHT . . . 39

CHAPTER 7
A HERO'S FAREWELL, A NEW JOURNEY BEGINS . . . 47

CHAPTER 8
STREET FIGHTING MAN . . . 52

CHAPTER 9
"SO YOU WANNA BOX, KID?" . . . 57

CHAPTER 10
MARVIN AND BERTHA . . . 63

CHAPTER 11
SUITCASE SAM ... 70

CHAPTER 12
BOSTON GARDEN ... 78

CHAPTER 13
CRAWLEY, ENGLAND ... 84

CHAPTER 14
MUNICH ... 89

CHAPTER 15
FRIDAY NIGHT FIGHTS ... 97

CHAPTER 16
HAGLER–SEALES II ... 104

CHAPTER 17
CUTS SLOW DOWN MINTER ... 108

CHAPTER 18
MINTER ON THE MOVE ... 117

CHAPTER 19
PHILLY ... 123

CHAPTER 20
HEARTBREAK AND REDEMPTION ... 130

CHAPTER 21
BECOMING MARVELOUS ... 138

CHAPTER 22
VINNIE CURTO ... 145

CHAPTER 23
CORRUPTION, SCANDAL, AND DON KING . . . 151

CHAPTER 24
STRENGTHENING "THE TRIANGLE" . . . 158

CHAPTER 25
BACK TO THE SPECTRUM . . . 163

CHAPTER 26
CONGRESSIONAL INTERVENTION . . . 169

CHAPTER 27
VITO "THE MOSQUITO" . . . 176

CHAPTER 28
TRAGEDY FOR MINTER . . . 181

CHAPTER 29
WORLD CHAMPION ALAN MINTER . . . 187

CHAPTER 30
THE NATIONAL FRONT . . . 194

CHAPTER 31
WAR OF WORDS IN LONDON . . . 199

CHAPTER 32
THE FIGHT . . . 205

CHAPTER 33
"A NATIONAL DISGRACE" . . . 212

EPILOGUE . . . 218

ACKNOWLEDGMENTS . . . 223

INTERVIEWS . . . 225

SOURCES . . . 227

Author's Note
This book is based on actual events reconstructed through hundreds of hours of research, the review of thousands of news stories, videos, court documents, and public records, plus more than fifty interviews over two years. In some instances, dialogue has been recreated for dramatic effect based on interviews, research, and historical fact.

"You have to starve the doubt and feed the faith"
—Marvelous Marvin Hagler

NEWARK

Newark, New Jersey, 1967

"Buddy, put out that candle and get down," Ida Mae Hagler told her brother, Eugene "Buddy" Monroe.

They were standing in the living room of Ida's third-floor apartment in a four-family brick building on war-torn Seymour Avenue in Newark. Outside, the worst riots in the city's history, and some of the deadliest in American history, raged. It was martial law.

Residents of Newark's Central Ward, almost all Black, were ordered to stay inside, or face arrest—or worse—from the throng of police and military lining the streets. Lights were turned off in every house so the cops outside wouldn't see movement inside. Any sudden movements were generally met with immediate gunfire from security forces trying desperately to end the killing, squash the bloody uprising, and regain control of the city.

No sooner had the words come out of Ida Mae's mouth than a bullet smashed through the window and embedded into the wall of the house. The single mother screamed, dove to the floor, and covered her babies' heads.

"Buddy!" she shouted.

Buddy also dove to the floor. No one was struck, miraculously. Sirens wailed outside and more gunfire erupted. It was a war zone.

"Lord, watch over us," the thirty-year-old mother of six said through tears, pulling her youngest tight to her body as they all cowered in fear on the rug.

Ida's oldest, thirteen-year-old Marvin lay next to his siblings—Veronica, Cheryl, Genarra, Noreen, and Robbie—his face buried in the floor as he listened to the gunshots pinging off the walls. His sisters screamed as Marvin tried his best to keep cool, despite being every bit as terrified as his brothers and sisters.

Marvin was the de facto man of the house, as there was no father in the home. Robert Sims Sr., the father of the four youngest children, had abandoned the family, leaving Ida Mae alone to fend for herself and raise her children in a violent city wracked by crime, drugs, and crooked cops.

Ida Mae had several men in and out of her life, including Marvin's biological father, who was never a big part of his life. Marvin's first wife, Bertha, said he rarely spoke about his dad. She said she only met him once when they were young.

Veronica, almost exactly a year younger than Marvin, says she had a different father. She said her father was a soldier who fought in World War II and Korea who struggled with his mental health.

"He was never the same after he came back [from the war]," she recalled.

According to her, he went to get medication at Newark General Hospital, climbed up to the sixth floor, and leaped out a window to his death.

Robert Sims Sr., an aspiring doo-wop singer, started dating Ida Mae when she was just fifteen. They married in 1956 and had four children together: Cheryl aka "Sherry," Robert Jr., Genarra, and Noreen, nicknamed "Buttons." Sims also had a child named Sharon from a previous relationship who also lived with the family.

Veronica and Marvin clung to each other as kids. They rode tricycles together. They explored the weed-strewn vacant lots in their neighborhood. They occasionally explored abandoned buildings and factories, many of which bore the fiery scars of civil uprising and urban warfare.

Ida struggled with the lack of support from the men who'd fathered her children. Robert Sims Sr. worked at a pickle factory while pursuing his singing career. Ida found occasional work as a housekeeper but had her hands full caring for the kids.

When Robert left, she took in Sharon as her own and was left to raise six kids. It was an impossible situation, as she had little income. She relied on government assistance and support from a few good friends and relatives, including her parents, as she tried to keep herself and her kids safe in a city brimming with dysfunction. She was a devoutly religious woman, which carried her through the dark times.

The once-proud city of Newark was crumbling under the weight of horrific violence, economic despair, racial strife, and corruption. Just a short drive from New York City, Newark should have been thriving but instead had become an economic disaster and an American tragedy. In 1967, it was the center of America's race war, wracked by postwar economic failures, white flight, failing schools, drugs, gangs, and police brutality.

Marvin grew numb to the chaos, alcoholism, and addiction that surrounded him. He became a loner, choosing to keep his head down and his mouth shut to avoid conflict in those angry streets. To cope with his loneliness, he started saving wounded birds. He built a coop on the roof of their building where he kept pigeons as friends. He once found a pet turtle, which he kept on the fire escape and sometimes put in the bathroom tub, much to his mother's dismay, especially when it was bath time for his baby brothers and sisters.

"They were the only friends I could relate to," Hagler said of the animals. "Maybe the only friends I really liked. I was always by myself."

The only men in Marvin's life at that time were his mother's brothers, James "Uncle Brother" Monroe and Eugene "Uncle Buddy" Monroe. Both lived up the street and were the closest thing Marvin had to a father figure in those days in Newark. Uncle Brother was in and out of prison, which only fueled young Marvin's anger and distrust of authority. It was, to say the least, a neighborhood devoid of hope. Marvin was scared, angry, and mostly alone.

Despite being surrounded by poverty and crime, their house was one of love and lots of good times. Veronica and Marvin were inseparable as they played innocently in junk-strewn vacant lots and streets, their childhood naivete protecting them from fear of the societal decay around them. They played marbles. Marvin loved to draw.

They were the Black version of Irish twins—just a bit more than a year apart—and had little adult supervision. They looked out for each other every day in an environment rife with danger.

While Ida Mae did not have much money, she knew fun was free. Every Halloween, she decorated the house as spookily as she could, enlisting her kids to help her draw bats, witches, pumpkins, spiders, and spiderwebs—anything to help create the spirit of Halloween. When Marvin and Veronica were seven and six, respectively, she threw a neighborhood Halloween party for the kids and their parents. All the kids came and most of them only had a mother, Veronica remembered.

Ida Mae strung up lights and hung the homemade decorations. The kids did such a good job that some of the mothers had to cradle their kids and assure them it was safe.

"Kid were scared to come up," Veronica recalled with a laugh. "Those were good times."

At Christmas, Ida Mae would sometimes get a bonus from one of the wealthy homeowners whose houses she cleaned. She always seemed to find a way to get the kids what they needed and put food on the table. Christmas dinners were always bountiful, even if her bank account was lean.

Their humble, close-knit lifestyle was in stark contrast to the complex socioeconomic disaster occurring outside their door. Smiles and laughs were often suddenly cut off abruptly when bullets rang out or sirens wailed. It was no way for a child to grow up, but Ida Mae's love was steadfast and she somehow managed to keep the kids safe.

Her survival instincts had been well developed by that time. She herself had a difficult road in her formative years, as she and her family migrated north to escape the depression of rural coal-mining towns in the South.

Ida Mae was born on June 17, 1937, in Logan, West Virginia, the oldest of two daughters of Bessie Monroe Alexander and Luther Hagler. Bessie was born in Chattanooga, Tennessee, and was also one of two sisters. The family were descendants of slaves who worked the bottomland of the Warrior River near Argo, Alabama.

Bessie quit school in fourth grade to help her younger sister and sick mother. She taught herself to read and write but life turned tragic when her mother and sister died. With no father, she was sent to live with an aunt in West Virginia.

There, she met Luther Hagler. They got married and had Ida Mae and her younger sister, Amy, nicknamed "Tiny." Luther and Bessie moved the family to Newark in 1941, but they divorced and Bessie remarried James Monroe. She and James moved with the girls to Fayetteville, North Carolina, where they had Ida's younger brothers, James and Eugene.

Bessie worked in a kitchen on the US Army base at Fort Bragg. With her mother working long hours, Ida Mae grew into a maternal role at a young age, helping cook for the young family. After Bessie and James divorced in 1947, Bessie moved back to Newark with all four kids in tow. She opened a soul-food restaurant in Newark's Central Ward where Ida Mae worked.

"I was so small I had to stand on a box in front of the stove," Ida Mae recalled.

When she was just sixteen, and with little education, Ida Mae became pregnant with her firstborn, Marvin, who was born on May 23, 1954—just as the US was seeking to exit the Korean War. Three days before Marvin's birth, Puerto Rican Olympic boxer Angel Figueroa, a member of the 223rd Infantry Regiment of the US Army, was killed at "The Punchbowl" in Korea, an infamous battleground during the war. It was a devastating casualty for Puerto Rico—and the boxing world—that rocked the nation and made global headlines.

At the time, boxing and baseball were America's top sports. The stars of the diamond and the squared circle were icons across the nation in those days. Little did the boxing world know that just three days after Figuerora's death, one of the world's future greats was born in a hospital in Newark.

Ida Mae was excited and hopeful about her newborn son, despite still being a child herself. She fell in love with the boy and they built a special bond.

As the young family grew, Marvin became the man of the house. With no father around, he was forced to put aside his own childhood to help raise his brothers and sisters.

"As long as we have each other, we can make it," Ida Mae used to tell him.

She preached several mantras to encourage Marvin and his siblings to be smart and stay safe: *Don't get on the wrong track: no drugs, no prisons for us. Stay away from strangers. Mind your own business. Come straight home from school. Stay home till I get home.*

"That's what brought us up to be the way we are," Marvin recalled years later. "Everybody that came into the house, you better make sure it was 'miss' or 'mister' when you spoke. That's the way she was."

She also had a rule for Marvin: he would not be allowed back into the house if he lost a street fight. After he got beaten up by one bully, Ida Mae took on the role of father and laid into her teenage son. She leaned down to him, her thick glasses just inches from the teenager's bruised face.

"Marvin, if you let them beat you one time, they'll do it again," she said. "Do not let them think you're a coward or they will do it again."

It was a harsh lesson for a young man with no father, but it was one that would stick with him for life.

Fighting for survival in the streets and under pressure to help his mother feed and clothe him and his siblings, things got harder for Marvin when his then-girlfriend had a baby and he took it upon himself to help her raise the boy. He was just fourteen. Marvin dropped out of high school and went to work at a local toy factory. While kids just a few miles away played high school football, went to proms, and planned for college, Marvin was lost in a cloud of fatherlessness. His only mentor, besides his uncles, was a local social worker named Mister Joe, who gave Marvin his first boxing lessons.

"He helped me with any problems I had," Hagler told *Sports Illustrated*. "He taught me sports. We went to the park to fly kites. He'd call up, 'What's the problem? You gonna be at the club?' He kept me out of trouble. He got me involved in counseling other kids."

Aimless and unsure of his future, Marvin helped his mother with the younger kids, worked, and tended to his animals, avoiding the rugged streets as much as possible. Like many young Black kids in Newark, he was angry. But he was not stupid. He knew the streets were a dead end. He also knew why activists and revolutionaries in his neighborhood and across America were fighting back against injustice, racism, and oppression. He knew very well why the powder keg outside his windows was detonating.

He heard the adults talking. He knew about white cops beating and shooting Black men in his neighborhood. He heard about the politicians who were not helping families in the Central Ward climb out of poverty and debt. He knew about the wealthy white business owners who paid workers peanuts and shut down factories and offices in poor neighborhoods when economic and political winds shifted.

Marvin also knew full well about racist landlords who refused to fix properties and let poor Black families live in squalor. He knew about banks refusing to give mortgages and business loans to Blacks. He knew what "redlining" was. He heard the old men in the neighborhood angrily ranting about corruption and systemic failings of the white political establishment ruling Newark. He heard his Uncle Brother talk about the prison-industrial complex and New Jersey's inhumane penitentiaries.

Marvin was young, but he was not a kid. He was wise to the ways of the world from a young age. And he was not surprised when the match was put to the fuse in Newark.

SUMMER OF '67

The so-called "Long, Hot Summer of '67," took its toll on Ida Mae. She was working part-time as a housekeeper in nearby Orange, New Jersey, and moonlighted as a server for a caterer. But, with six kids to support, it seemed the money she made was never enough.

There were tough times, but Ida always found a way.

"As long as I've got you, I'm a rich woman," she often told the kids.

For Marvin and his siblings, living in poverty was normal. All their neighbors were poor and they were surrounded by crime. Still, it was a mostly happy home. They knew their mother loved them and would do anything to make sure they were fed and safe.

But in the summer of 1967, Newark erupted in violence. Protecting her family became almost impossible. There were more than 150 uprisings in cities across America that summer as the nation's first racial reckoning unfolded in destruction and chaos from Watts to Newark to Atlanta to Birmingham to Boston. It was a time of tumult and revolt across America. The war in Vietnam caused deep divides that were exacerbated along racial, socioeconomic, and generational lines.

The deindustrialization of American cities, especially blue-collar ones like Newark, left millions of Blacks unemployed and without quality housing, education, and job training, all while thousands of young men were shipped off to fight a doomed mission against the Viet Cong. With poverty, war, and despair came increased drugs and violence in cities like Newark, as well as rampant racial profiling and police brutality.

Racial tensions across America had never been higher, triggered initially by a violent Black rebellion in Los Angeles' Watts neighborhood. Newark was locked in a post-World War II downward spiral as whites fled the city for the suburbs in record numbers, leaving behind depressed communities filled with Blacks and a bitter white power structure.

Newark had a large Italian population and was one of the first American cities settled by immigrants from Italy. As white flight took hold and poor Black families moved in, resentment and anger grew between the Italian families who would not—or could not—move out and the poor Black families moving in. Racism was rampant and many of the cops on the Newark police force were Italians who carried that bitterness onto the beat every day.

Newark, more than most American cities, was poised to explode.

On the night of July 17, it did just that.

Around 9:40 p.m., a struggling trumpet player and cab driver from Salisbury, North Carolina, named John William Smith picked up a fare near Newark City Hospital.

Smith, forty, had recently moved to a one-bedroom apartment in Newark's Ironbound District to pursue a music career. He had spent that day visiting nightclubs where he hoped to perform before going to his night-shift job as a cab driver.

Smith was a US Army veteran who served in Japan and the Philippines during World War II and in Korea during the Korean War. Before joining the military he attended North Carolina Agricultural and Technical State College and went to music school in New York.

He took the cabbie job to help make ends meet while pursuing his music career, and also to pay off dental bills after getting his two front teeth fixed. He wasn't the best cabbie, and in fact was driving with a revoked license that night because of a string of fender-benders he had been in during the previous week.

As he drove on 15th Avenue, he saw a police cruiser double-parked. He flicked the directional and pulled around the cruiser, catching the attention of the two white Italian cops sitting inside. Officers John DeSimone and Vito Pontrelli hit the lights and siren and sped after Smith.

Smith pulled over. The officers approached the cab and told him he ran the intersection. They demanded that he exit the cab.

"What's going on?" Smith asked.

"Step out of the car," DeSimone said.

Smith's female passenger told the officers she was late for an appointment. They told her to get out of the vehicle and sent her along her way to get another cab.

Things then turned confrontational and the two cops started pummeling Smith with their fists and nightsticks.

"I was just disgusted because I was losing my fare," Smith later told his North Carolina hometown newspaper, *The Salisbury Post*. "Then they went to work on me."

They threw him into the back of the cruiser and continued thrashing him as they drove to the Fourth Precinct. As the cruiser pulled up, residents of Hayes Homes, a housing project across the street from the station, saw the cops drag Smith's nearly unconscious body inside, where he was beaten some more.

"By the time we got to the Fourth Precinct, I was immobile," Smith remembered. "They was dragging me into the station and a woman yelled, 'You don't have to drag him like that.'"

Inside the station, the beating continued.

"About ten of those dudes went to work on me and dumped me in a cell," Smith recalled. "I wanted to go to the hospital. I had broken ribs. I was beat in the head. I had my jaw broke. I was worked over."

While Smith lay bloodied and beaten in a cell, outside gathered an angry mob, exhausted by systemic oppression and furious at the city's failure to rein in bad cops. Someone tossed a rock through the precinct window. Others started throwing bricks and bottles. Officers in riot gear burst out of the station and started clubbing protesters. An unruly crowd stormed City Hall.

Ironically, a protest had already been planned for that night in response to the outbreaks of violence across the country that summer. When the rocks and bottles started flying at the Fourth Precinct, word quickly spread around the city and well-prepared protesters sprang into action. It was a perfect storm of chaos in a fraught city ripe for an explosion.

The violence was relatively contained that night, but the next day, the city exploded. A rally outside the precinct turned violent again, touching off five straight nights of bloodshed that claimed the lives of twenty-six people.

Cops and protesters clashed all over Newark as thousands of bullets from cops and National Guard soldiers pierced the air, day and night, killing mothers, fathers, sons and daughters. Fires raged and stores were looted. More than seven hundred people were wounded and fifteen hundred were arrested.

Marvin, like everyone else in the neighborhood, learned quickly about the beating police laid on a poor, unsuspecting cabbie. He was not surprised when the neighborhood erupted and the city lurched into chaos, leading to some of the deadliest and most destructive rioting in US history.

It was a familiar scene to Marvin. The only white people he knew in Newark were teachers, cops, and politicians—and in his experience none of them were friends to the Black community.

He was raised in a community that justifiably distrusted government and the justice system. They lived in shoddy housing and attended failing schools. With no father to protect him, teach him, help him—like many other young men in the neighborhood—he fully understood the anger outside his windows. He felt it too.

He saw his mother struggle. Ida Mae showered her children with love but the darkness of that summer of violence in Newark had her at her breaking point.

Among those killed during the rioting was Eloise Spellman, a mother of eleven felled by a bullet that ripped through their tenth-floor apartment. Eddie Moss, a ten-year-old boy riding with his family home from White Castle in a station wagon, was also killed by a stray bullet.

Newark Police Officer Frederick Toto, a thirty-three-year-old father of three, was gunned down by a rooftop sniper. And twelve-year-old Michael Pugh, a sixth grader who was just starting a summer job, was killed by a bullet as he sat on his front steps. The death toll was staggering. The number of mothers and children killed and injured stunned Ida Mae and made her fearful for the lives of herself and her children.

"Stay away from the windows," she told Marvin and his younger brothers and sisters as gunshots rang out night after night.

Police and National Guardsmen were everywhere—on the street, on the rooftops—chasing looters and searching for snipers. There were reports of cops shooting people indiscriminately as they ran down the street, some of whom were innocent and simply seeking cover.

The Hagler family could hear the footsteps of the troops running across the rooftop above their third-floor apartment. Marvin looked down and saw looters carrying stolen goods, rifle-toting cops in pursuit.

"Get back from those windows!" Ida Mae shouted, startling her oldest son. "I don't want any of you kids standing up. Stay down."

She knew about the nurse's aide down the street who was struck and killed by a police officer's bullet that tore through her house as she approached a window to protect her two-year-old daughter.

For several days, Ida Mae and the kids laid on the floor, sleeping side-by-side and only moving around the apartment on all fours. They were prisoners in their own home as cops patrolled the streets outside, firing at random and often getting into gun battles with rooftop snipers and other civilians joining in the uprising.

Ida Mae and the kids stayed out of the line of fire, sliding across the floor on couch cushions to get to the bathroom and the kitchen.

"It was like the end of the world," Veronica remembers.

"Mom, we need to get out of here," Marvin told his mother.

More bullets rang off the house.

"I know baby," she said. "I know."

For Marvin and his family, it was the start of a tumultuous two years that frequently resulted in gunplay outside their house. Newark was teetering on the brink of collapse. The white political power structure excoriated the Black community for the uprising. Conversely, Black leaders blamed the cops and explained that the violence was a natural response to years of oppression and injustice.

"I'm sorry about the rupture of black-and-white feelings and relationships in our town,"

Sally Carrol, the president of the Newark NAACP, told the Hackensack, New Jersey *Record*: "I think we can correct the evils without burning, killing, and looting. But on the other hand, we at the NAACP have been trying to do that for fifty years, haven't we? And nothing has happened."

Dr. Nathan Wright, a Harvard-educated minister in Newark, was more direct, saying: "Nonviolence has failed. The only thing the white man in

Newark will respond to is the threat of violence and certain promise that the threat is not an empty one."

During those days, Marvin's future looked bleak. He became bitter and withdrew more and more to the pigeons in his coop to avoid engaging in the anger permeating his community.

When the violence subsided, Marvin and his sisters would sometimes walk thirty minutes across town to visit their grandparents. Other days, they would walk to the corner store and see their uncles.

Uncle Brother would buy the kids snacks and treats at the corner store. Marvin looked up to both of his uncles because they were around more than any of the fathers he knew in his family, and also because they were both extremely physically fit. Marvin talked to Uncle Brother a lot about how to sculpt his body. He learned from a young age how to eat right, exercise, and be disciplined about his fitness from his uncles. They were lessons he carried throughout his life.

However, there was more heartache and tragedy to come.

The violence that summer was only the beginning as both sides dug in. The fact that the officers who arrested and beat John William Smith were Italian was not lost on the Black community. Newark's Italian community had deep roots in the city. While Italians flowed into New York City's burgeoning Little Italy in the late 1800s, filling the flats on Mulberry Street and surrounding neighborhoods, another Little Italy was popping up in Newark's First Ward. It was one of the central ports in the great Italian Migration that started in the 1870s and included more than four million Italians finding their way to the United States, most to the Northeast.

The Italian enclave in Newark grew after Angelo Maria Mattia and twenty-seven other Italian immigrants landed in New York from the town of Calabritto in Italy's Avellino Province. While looking for work, Mattia and the others got on the wrong ferry and landed in Newark, where they found an open job market in a new neighborhood they called "Nevarca."

The city was heavily Irish then, but by 1920 Newark had the fifth-highest Italian population in the United States. They were cobblers, masons, fishmongers, grocers, restaurateurs, funeral directors, bakers, and, eventually, cops, firefighters, and politicians.

New York Yankees great Joe DiMaggio famously took his teammates to Seventh Avenue in Newark to experience real Italian cuisine, while Frank Sinatra had his bread delivered from Newark's Giordano's Bakery weekly until his final days. Frankie Valli grew up there.

After World War II, however, the city changed rapidly. Misguided, and ultimately failed, urban-renewal efforts orchestrated by the federal government to provide housing to poor Blacks resulted in thousands of Italians being evicted from their apartments, as buildings were razed to make way for massive housing complexes. The construction of the New Jersey Turnpike, Interstate 280, and I-78 only made things worse, tearing through ethnic enclaves—mostly Italian—and further dividing the community.

A breaking point for the Italian-American community came when the federal government financed a massive project to tear down forty-six-acres of occupied tenement housing—labeled a slum—that was replaced with high-rise, multiunit housing. It was a catastrophic event as thousands of Italian families were evicted and poor, mostly Black, families moved in.

As urban blight grew, so did the discord. The Italian community rapidly migrated out of the First Ward and Seventh Avenue as the Black community grew. The racial makeup of the city changed seemingly overnight. During the 1950s, more than a hundred thousand whites fled Newark, replaced by more than sixty thousand Blacks. Newark's Black population between 1940 and 1970 went from just 10 percent to more than 54 percent. No other American city had ever seen such a rapid racial shift. The impact of such rapidly changing neighborhoods caused some of the most intense racial divisions in US history. The Newark police department had fourteen hundred cops but in 1967, when the riots erupted, just one hundred fifty of them were nonwhite.

The feud between the Italians and Blacks in Newark and the 1967 riots was so pronounced and intense that it was a backdrop for the 2021 film, *The Many Saints of Newark*, a prequel to the *The Sopranos*. Marvin could have easily been a character in that film. He grew up immersed in the Italian-versus-Black narrative, hearing about it in school, on the stoop of his home from elderly Black men, and in vitriol spewed by old Italian men who did not hide their disdain for poor Blacks like Marvin and his family.

Leroi Jones, an acclaimed Black playwright and poet who later changed his name to Amiri Bakara, grew up in Newark while the city's racial transition unfolded. He saw firsthand how Italians in Newark clashed with Blacks. Many Italians believed they were being marginalized and pushed out. Many felt the very soul of their city was being stolen from them.

Jones blamed the riots on jaded, angry, and racist Italian cops. The burgeoning activist and writer was among the thousands arrested during the riots. His crime was illegally carrying a gun, which he admittedly brandished because the streets had become war zones. Like most arrested during the uprising, Jones was beaten senseless.

"I recognized the Italian cop who arrested me," Jones said. "I knew him from high school. He called me a 'black nigger animal' and busted me on the side of my head."

"This ain't nothing new man," he continued. "We been in an ass-kicking fight with these wop cats for years. These wop mothers took this town from the Irish. Now, baby, we going to take it from them."

The fallout from the riots continued for years and white flight intensified.

John William Smith, the cabbie whose arrest touched off three years of unrest, moved back to North Carolina and worked construction. In 1969, he went on trial for assaulting the two officers. He was convicted and sentenced to prison for three years. He remained free pending appeal and filed a lawsuit alleging bias and "discrimination" in the courts because Blacks were underrepresented on juries in New Jersey. According to the suit, Blacks made up 25 percent of the population of Essex County, where Newark is located, but only 6 percent of juries. The fourteen-person jury that convicted Smith was composed of all white men, mostly upper-middle-class professionals.

It took five years before Smith's conviction was overturned by a federal appeals court in Philadelphia. Lawyers for the State of New Jersey denied bias in the jury-selection process and tried to bring Smith's case to the US Supreme Court, but the high court refused to hear the pleadings and upheld the Appeals Court ruling, setting Smith free once and for all. It was a hollow victory.

Smith never went back to Newark and lived out his life in North Carolina. He died April 5, 2002, at the age of seventy-five.

The cops who arrested and beat him, meanwhile, faced no sanctions. This was typical in the '60s and was why Marvin always listened to Ida and Uncle Brother when they warned him about police in the neighborhood.

BROCKTON

Two years later, in 1969, more violence erupted in Newark. The nonstop bloodshed in poor American cities like Newark was the antithesis of the "flower power" movement hippies were singing about in parks and at music festivals.

The media focused on Woodstock, Haight-Ashbury, the Beatles, the Rolling Stones, and the exploding hippie culture, largely ignoring the fact that American cities—and specifically Black communities like Newark—were becoming battlefields. But beyond the Vietnam protests and the hippie demonstrations on college campuses and at political rallies, there was a simmering movement afoot in the ghettos of America that summer. It was an uprising of poor Blacks who were tired of oppression, underfunded and crumbling schools, rundown housing, no economic opportunity, and living in police states.

For two nights in 1969, thousands of Blacks once again roamed the streets of Newark, smashing store windows, looting, and hurling bottles at police cars. The anger surrounded Marvin and his family again. They were terrified. There were more arrests and gunshots, but no one was killed. But back were the police sirens, the gunfire, the chaos. The cops once again lined the streets. Once again, the Hagler kids became prisoners in their own home.

Ida Mae had seen enough. After school ended that June, she decided riot-plagued Newark was no place to raise her family. She needed a change and a better life for her kids.

A few months earlier, her sister, Amy "Tiny" Thomas, had moved to California. Tiny was a go-go dancer in Newark. The kids recalled seeing her come over to chat with her sister before her shifts at a local nightclub, where she danced in cages up on stage. It was not the best work, but Tiny liked it and it paid her rent.

Tiny worked hard and raised her kids dancing on those stages. It's also where she met the man who would take her out of Newark and convince her to start a new life in California.

Ida was heartbroken when her only sister moved, but she understood the reasoning. She was happy her sister went to start a new life on the West Coast, far from the violence of Newark. Once Tiny left, there was little debate for Ida over leaving Newark. It was just a matter of when and where she would rebuild her life as a single mother with six kids.

She reached out to family in search of a lifeline. She found it from a cousin in a medium-sized city in Massachusetts that she knew little about: Brockton.

One day that summer, she brought Marvin, his little brother Robbie, and their sister Gennara, to the bus station, paid their fare and packed them onto a bus bound for Brockton. Marvin, just fifteen, was in charge. He and his younger siblings made it to Brockton while Ida, Veronica, and Cheryl drove north on Interstate 95 in a rented moving truck packed with all of the family's belongings.

Marvin and the kids were met at the bus station by Ida's Aunt Cat. She and her husband, Earl, lived in a public housing project on North Main Street in Brockton, which is where Marvin's post-Newark life began.

Marvin had never been to Brockton before that day. He knew nothing about it. His sister Cheryl recalls the kids being upset that they were uprooted from Newark. The kids knew there was violence in Newark but to them it was home. It was where their friends were, and they had fond memories of playing in the vacant lots and going to summer camps. Plus their grandparents stayed behind in Newark.

"I was so disappointed because I was moved away from my friends that I grew up with," says Cheryl.

Marvin and his siblings dropped off their bags in Aunt Cat's apartment and waited for their mother to arrive. Uncle Earl and Aunt Cat did not have much. It was a two-bedroom, one-bathroom apartment in a modest public housing complex, but it was clean and safe. They made Marvin and the kids feel welcome.

Ida, Cheryl, and Veronica arrived a few days later. A blue-collar city of one hundred thousand people, Brockton has had ups-and-downs over the last fifty years with respect to violence and gangs, but, in 1969, it was a far safer community than Newark, especially for a young single mother with two boys. And there were jobs.

It was close quarters for the family, but they made it work in the small apartment, sharing meals, playing board games, and watching *The Mod Squad*, *Rowan & Martin's Laugh-In*, and other TV shows together. Best of all there were no military police or bonfires burning outside their windows.

Ida went back to school to get her GED. She got a driver's license. She got a job cleaning houses and catering events while the kids enrolled in Brockton schools—except for Marvin, who went to work in construction as a laborer.

His younger siblings had to get physicals and certifications for vaccines before they could be enrolled so Ida Mae spent a lot of time those first few weeks getting the younger kids settled in their new schools.

Marvin's pay helped keep the family afloat during those early days in Brockton. He did not mind working but he was lost in a new city with an obligation to help support his brothers and sisters.

He had no money, holes in his beat-up canvas tennis sneakers, and a chip on his shoulder the size of New Jersey as he considered what kind of life he was going to have. He also was suddenly thrust into a racially-mixed city. In his Newark neighborhood, there were no whites, but Brockton was a melting pot of Italians, Irish, Lithuanians, Jews, and Blacks.

"The only times I had dealt with whites, they were owners of stores or in positions of authority," Marvin recalled years later. "I didn't know how to accept them or trust them as friends. I was suspicious."

While he acclimated to this strange new existence, two time zones away, another Brocktonian was about to learn his fate—one that would impact Marvin for the rest of his life.

GOODY AND ROCKY

On August 31, 1969, Guerino "Goody" Petronelli had no idea who Marvin Hagler was. Goody had just been discharged from the US Navy after a nineteen-year career.

He was driving from California back to Brockton with big plans. He and his brother, Pasquale, aka Pat, started training boxers and opened a small gym in 1965. They were planning to have their friend Rocky Marciano, the recently-retired heavyweight champion, work with them training young boxers.

The only undefeated heavyweight champion in history, Rocky retired abruptly from boxing in 1956. In those days, there were two sports that mattered in America—baseball and boxing. If you were the heavyweight champion of the world, you were one of the most famous and celebrated people on the planet, and that's what Rocky was in those years.

He was a sports superstar and a pop-culture icon who hung around the Hollywood elite, but deep down he always remained a blue-collar kid from Brockton, the son of an Italian factory worker. He lived his life humbly and conservatively, as though he were always one step away from working in the factories himself. Sure, he liked nice clothes, his pool in Florida, and hanging out with movie stars and entertainers. But he never forgot how hard his family had to work for him to have the opportunity at the life he had. And there was nothing that was going to take that from him.

After Rocky won his last fight and retired, the Petronelli brothers started talking with their friend about his post-boxing plans. The brothers were opening a gym in Brockton and Rocky would be their ambassador. Rocky was reluctant; running a gym was never in his plans. But he did love the sport and adored his hometown. He agreed to lend his name to the gym and work with young fighters—not only to help his longtime friends, but also to give something back to the city that gave him so much.

For the Petronelli brothers, the partnership ensured they would not only get best prospects from Brockton, but also fighters from Providence, Boston, Lawrence, Lowell, and the other fighting cities in the region. The brothers were in heated competition with the Ward 5 Gym, which was run by fellow Italian-American boxing manager/trainer Vinnie Vecchione, who was bankrolled by a mobbed-up bar owner named Matthew "Gigi" Sergio. There was no love lost between the two camps and the Petronellis knew that having Rocky on their side would give them a significant advantage—not only in attracting fighters, but securing lucrative matches for their stable of contenders. Rocky had star power, but he was also on a first-name basis with promoters around New England, not to mention most of the mobsters who ran the business behind the scenes.

Goody was excited for the new venture with his famous friend when he left Los Alamitos Naval Air Station, bound for home. Goody had completed his military service—which included serving during World War II in the South Pacific—and was looking forward to civilian life and, hopefully, success in boxing.

As his Pontiac rumbled along a North Dakota highway, he thought of home. Brockton was always home, and now he had a plan to not only make his life there, but also do something positive for the community and the kids in the city he loved. And maybe make a few bucks.

He was content putting his military life behind him, including his own boxing career that was long ago ended by a shattered hand. This was a new start.

His introspective cross-country road trip was abruptly interrupted, though, when a news alert came over the car's AM radio.

"We have a breaking news report," the announcer said. "We are sorry to report that there has been a horrible plane crash today in Iowa. One of the passengers was boxing great, Rocky Marciano. Mr. Marciano is dead."

Goody was stunned and nearly drove off the road. He swerved and drove a bit more in shock before pulling into a coffee shop to gather his thoughts.

Rocky, the most recognizable heavyweight in boxing, along with Muhammad Ali, and one of the most famous athletes in the world, was gone. Just like that.

For Goody, it was unfathomable. He walked over to the pay phone in the coffee shop and called his brother Pat.

"Pat," he said.

"I know," Pat said somberly through the receiver.

"What are we going to do?" Goody said.

Around the corner from Pat, Rocky's younger brother Peter lay in his bed sleeping. He had just finished his bartending shift at the Holiday Inn at the Westgate Mall in Brockton and was sound asleep at 1:30 a.m. when the phone rang.

"When the phone rings at that time of night, it's not good news," Peter Marciano recalls.

It was Hank Tartaglia, a longtime family friend whose cousin, Anthony "Snap" Tartaglia, was an amateur boxer and one of Rocky's cornermen. The Tartaglia family was well-known in Brockton for owning and operating George's Cafe, a popular Italian family restaurant, for generations. The wood-paneled, smoky eatery served up delicious bar pizza and a variety of Italian red-sauce classics, drawn from family recipes. George's was a gathering spot for the Italian community in Brockton and was the site of many of Rocky's post-fight celebrations. Throughout the decades, the Tartaglia family hosted parties for every fighter imaginable, including Muhammad Ali and, in later years, Marvelous Marvin Hagler.

"Buddy, you're awake right," Hank said.

"Yeah of course, I'm talking," Peter replied.

"I'm coming over to your house. I'm a few minutes away," Hank told him.

Hank was a bookmaker and hung around some rough characters, so Peter thought his friend was "in the jackpot," either with the law or possibly with a woman. Hank arrived at the house. When Peter opened the door, his friend had tears in his eyes.

"I just got word that Rocky was in a plane crash and he died," Hank told him.

Peter was stunned. He tried to compose himself, got dressed and drove over to his mother's house. When he arrived and told his mother and father the news, his mother collapsed, sobbing, and spoke in their native Italian.

"Figlio mio, il cuore della mia vita," she said.

"My son, the heart of my life."

"That sticks out in my mind. I think about it quite a bit," Peter says.

The Marciano family, as well as the Petronellis, were still grieving the tragic loss of Rocky's longtime trainer, Allie Colombo, who died just a few months earlier in a horrible industrial accident. Allie was Rocky's closest friend and was someone that he considered a huge part of his career.

"It was Allie's contention that I could make it very big in the professional ranks, so we talked it over together and decided to give it a try," Rocky told the press after Allie died. "Allie was a real buddy. He kept my interest in boxing alive through all the difficult moments. Prizefighting is a very serious business, but Allie was very witty and when we got too serious he'd use his sense of humor to relax the atmosphere."

Allie was a few years older than Goody and Rocky. He was the older kid who organized the pickup baseball games in James Edgar Playground across from Rocky's Dover Street house. The park was named after James Edgar, owner of Edgar's Department Store, which had the first-ever department-store Santa Claus, later made famous by Macy's in New York. The park, which is today outfitted with a plaque honoring Rocky, was where his brawling legend was born. It started with a legendary knockout against a local bully that showed Allie his friend's power for the first time.

"Rocky hit this kid with a right uppercut and he went right up on his toes and spun around and fell flat on his face. That was the first time we knew how hard Rocky could punch," Allie once recalled.

Himself an amateur boxer, Allie worked out with Rocky at the Brockton YMCA and was in his corner from day one as "The Rock" battled all comers in smoke-filled gyms and arenas across New England. Allie served eight years in the US Army and was planning a military career, but abruptly quit after seeing the punching power and ability of his buddy. He withdrew his life savings—$1,800—and staked it on Rocky's boxing career, paying for hotels, meals, and gas to get to fights.

After Rocky beat everyone from Brockton to Providence, he and Allie hitchhiked to Manhattan to showcase for managers. One of them was Al Weill, a one-time ballroom dancer and slick double-talker who was a manager and matchmaker. Rocky and Allie lived on sandwiches and stayed at a YMCA in Midtown while training hard for fights that came his way. They knew that beating the best in New England was good, but, to truly be a champion, you had to beat the best in New York.

"It was worth every sacrifice . . . it opened all the doors Rocky had to have open. I learned real quick you weren't going anywhere unless you fought in New York," Allie once said. "I made a deal with Weill . . . and that is how we got started."

Rocky always felt that without Allie, he would have led a much different life, most likely working in the Brockton shoe factories.

"I'd never have gotten where I did without him," Rocky once said.

Allie died January 6, 1969, at age forty-eight, when he was crushed by a tractor trailer that tipped over on top of him as he operated a forklift in a supermarket parking lot in the Readville section of Boston. The sudden tragedy hit Rocky hard.

"He saw my potential as a fighter and talked me into boxing," Rocky said after Allie's death. "He kept me interested in boxing at times when things weren't going good . . . He was with me from the very beginning."

Just as Rocky had to figure out his future without Allie, Goody and Pat were now faced with an uncertain future without Rocky.

ROCKY'S RISE

Born October 12, 1923, in Milford, Massachusetts, Guerino "Goody" Petronelli was one of twelve children of Italian immigrants. His father, Paul, was a mason who came from the Abruzzo region of Italy—just like Rocky. Goody's mother, Mary, was a homemaker. His brother, Pasquale "Pat" Petronelli, was two years older, born on October 15, 1921. The family moved to Brockton when the brothers were young.

Brockton, at the time, was a shoe manufacturing hub just twenty-two miles south of Boston and forty miles north of Providence. Like most American cities of that era, Brockton was a melting pot. In addition to a vibrant Italian community, there were French, Irish, Lithuanian, and Jewish neighborhoods, as well as a growing Black community that grew out of the city's status as a final stop on the Underground Railroad. Frederick Douglas held emancipation ceremonies at the Liberty Tree in downtown Brockton, which still stands today. The Black community worked alongside the Italians, Lithuanians, and Irish in the shoe shops and helped build Brockton. Today, Brockton is the only majority-Black city in New England.

Known as the "Shoe City," it was once the shoe manufacturing capital of the world with more than ninety factories. In the early and mid-1900s, it had a busy downtown with theaters, nightclubs, pool halls, restaurants, shops, and large department stores.

First settled by Myles Standish and other English colonizers in the mid-1600s on land occupied by the Wampanoag Native American tribe, Brockton was originally a part of the town of Bridgewater. It was originally known as North Bridgewater but was renamed in the late 1800s after Sir Isaac Brock, a British military general who fought in the War of 1812.

During the Civil War, Brockton was the largest supplier of shoes to the United States military. The city manufactured and delivered tens of thousands of boots to Union soldiers, including those who fought in the Battle of Gettysburg and other historic clashes. After the Civil War, the shoe industry thrived for decades, employing thousands and making the city an attractive place to work and raise a family. Footwear innovation took hold in Brockton in the late 1800s as the world's first left-and-right-designated pairs of shoes were created in the city, soon followed by the first automated shoe-manufacturing machines.

At the turn of the 20th century, the shoe industry employed as many as fifteen thousand workers in Brockton, in addition to thousands more at related manufacturing facilities. By World War I, it was one of the largest manufacturing hubs of military and retail footwear in the world, shipping shoes that sold for a then-outrageous five US dollars a pair in Cuba, Italy, Denmark, Belgium, France, and Mexico. In 1920, the industry took in $8 million a month in shoe sales, which is roughly $120 million today, adjusted for inflation. The city's population exploded from thirteen thousand in 1880 to nearly seventy thousand in 1920. Today it is home to 106,000 residents.

At the height of the city's industrial era, Thomas Edison, the godfather of electricity, chose Brockton for his first experimental laboratory. Edison tested many of his inventions in Brockton and, as a result, the city was home to the nation's first electrified fire station, factory, high school, and theater. The country's first underground electrical system was pioneered by Edison in Brockton and the city was home to the first-ever residential home powered by electricity. The city's innovation carried over to sports too, as the first catcher's mitt was invented in 1875 in Brockton by pro baseball player/manager Billy "Gunner" McGunnigle.

The Great Depression, however, hit the city hard. The shoe business declined in the 1930s as manufacturers moved operations to the South and Europe. Young men went off to war and women worked in the factories, supporting their families. In 1941, the city was home to one of the deadliest roof-collapse fires in US history, when thirteen firefighters died battling a massive blaze at The Strand Theater.

It was during the Great Depression that the Marchegiano and Petronelli families came of age on Brockton's West Side.

Goody and Pat were inseparable from birth, the closest of their parents' dozen kids. They played together, fought together, and navigated their way through Brockton together as young boys. Their father worked in the shoe factories, but also built a small construction business that provided supplemental income. During the Great Depression, times were of course tough. The family struggled and, like many during the era, relied on government assistance at times.

Postwar industrial America in a small city like Brockton was a simpler time, but it was not an easy life. Dust-and-debris-encrusted men and women toiled long, hard hours at the factories, their kids often running wild. Fathers and mothers left their kids at home while they trudged off to the factory to breathe in toxins and bathe in oil and chemicals making boots and shoes for the troops. The parents returned home exhausted, their faces smeared with industrial smudge. Many kids dropped out of school in those days to work alongside their parents in the factories as families struggled to make ends meet.

Paul Petronelli struck out on his own, building a construction company. While boxing fame was far from the Petronelli family's plans, Goody first stepped into a boxing ring at the age of ten.

"The Knights of Columbus had a gym in Brockton and there was ... a city boxing program," Goody said. "I just loved boxing ... I come from a large family of seven boys and five girls, so you had to know how to handle yourself."

In his high school yearbook, he listed his interests as: "football, baseball, skating, movies, dancing, reading, music, basketball." Nothing about boxing. His future, he wrote, was in "office work."

Following high school, both brothers joined the military. Pat joined the US Army and saw combat in World War II in Italy with the 88th Infantry Division's Blue Devils. He fought as an amateur and had twenty-seven fights before deciding he would rather make a living in business and construction, like his father, than in the ring.

Goody graduated from Brockton High in 1941 and joined the US Navy. He became a master chief petty officer and trained boxers at an airbase in Grosse Isle, Michigan. He was a poor, wiry Italian kid from outside Boston and there was no shortage of guys who wanted to challenge him in the Navy. So he turned to boxing and started training so he could defend himself. He fought as a welterweight and had an amateur record of 23-2-1.

He once fought in an amateur tournament called the Diamond Belt and had three bouts in the same day, knocking out all three opponents. It was a story he would share for the rest of his life, and one he would use to taunt Marvin in later years. He had twenty-seven pro fights, but his career ended after he shattered his right hand in a bout when he was just twenty-three.

When Goody was nineteen, he was serving on a Navy base in Wilmington, Delaware when he wandered into a small cafe and met a striking young Irish girl, Marian Gorman. She was just sixteen and still in high school. They started dating and Goody quickly realized he had found the love of his life.

They got married two years later, on May 10, 1943, just before Goody was deployed to the South Pacific during World War II. He served as a medic aboard the USS Bon Homme Richard off the coast of Japan as part of an American fleet that supported the atomic bomb attacks on Hiroshima and Nagasaki. Like too many American military members, he witnessed the carnage of the nuclear attack. He rarely spoke about it, but those close to him say it affected him until his final days.

After the nuclear attacks in Japan, Goody returned home but stayed enlisted in the military, later serving in both Korea and Vietnam.

In 1951, while stationed in Boston, he participated in a sea rescue after a plane crash in Dorchester Bay. He was stationed at the US Naval Base in Squantum, a section of Quincy, Massachusetts, when, on November 24, 1951, a Navy plane crashed into the ocean and sank about a mile offshore. Goody and his crew sprang into action. He was among several seamen who responded to the scene and were credited with saving Lieutenant J. G. McIlwee of Cambridge. Goody and eighteen fellow members of the Navy received a commendation for their heroics in December 1951.

The Petronelli and Marciano families were old-school Italians and fought for their families' survival day after day. Big families, big hearts, hard-working, and committed to family. Those were their values. Goody and Rocky became running buddies. While their parents worked, Goody and Rocky pulled pranks and hopped fences. They shot craps in back alleys, careful not to get caught by the local cops, or suffer the consequences from their no-nonsense fathers.

Rocky's father, Peirino Marchegiano, emigrated to the United States in 1912 from the town of Ripa Teatina in the Abruzzo region of Italy. Goody's father, Paul, who came from the same region of Italy, emigrated to the US around the same time. Both families settled in Brockton because it had jobs, housing, and lots of Italians.

Pierino enlisted in the US Marines in 1917 and fought for America in WWI, earning a Gold Star. But his wartime service took its toll. His platoon was hit with mustard gas, causing lifelong injuries that ultimately contributed to his death in 1973. Upon his honorable discharge in 1919, he went to work for Stacy Adams, one of Brockton's many shoe factories, toiling away to feed and house his family.

He was proud to work for Adams, which manufactured a higher-end shoe, and not Knapp Shoe, one of the city's biggest factories that made lower-cost, mass-produced footwear. Pierino worked five and a half days a week—Saturday overtime was pretty much standard—and the family had dinner at the same time every night. Five o'clock on the dot, dinner was ready when Pierino got home, showered, and sat down at the table. All six kids had better be washed and seated, unless they had a good excuse. It was a very strict routine that Pierino enforced because he knew that the ritual was vital to keeping his family connected and close.

A baseball and football star at Brockton High School, Rocky lived on Dover Street, a blue-collar enclave of mostly Italian families, with his parents and five brothers and sisters. The Petronellis were just a few streets away. The Italians stuck together. Those same mandatory family dinners took place nightly at the Petronelli home as well. It was a time when mothers and fathers yelled out the door for their kids to get home for dinner, and there were consequences for those who did not heed the call.

The Marchegiano home at 168 Dover Street was always buzzing with kids running in and out. The modest two-story home was a gathering spot for family and friends and became well known thanks to a homemade heavy bag that hung from a large oak tree in the front yard. Rocky pummeled it day after day, building the crushing overhand right that would one day be called "Suzie Q." The punch became his ticket to the heavyweight championship.

A five-foot-ten-inch, two-hundred-pound bull of a man, Rocky was a standout athlete who seemed destined to be a baseball star. He was cut from the Brockton High School team, though, because he broke league rules when he joined a church-league team. He was angry and crestfallen, as his heroes were Babe Ruth and Lou Gehrig. He was so distraught that he quit school and went to work as a laborer while playing semipro baseball.

He was a catcher and a natural athlete and once had a tryout with the Chicago Cubs, but he did not impress the team's brass. He could hit for power but could not throw from home plate to second with any accuracy, so baseball was out. His destiny, instead, lay in the ring. But not before he was recruited into the military during World War II.

In 1943, Rocky was drafted into the US Army. Like his friends Goody and Pat, he was shipped overseas. Rocky was stationed in Wales where he worked on the docks, shipping weapons and supplies to the troops in Normandy. On the base, he was challenged because of his brawn and tough-guy demeanor. So he, too, took up boxing. He won the 1946 Armed Forces amateur title.

The title only built his reputation as a tough guy and led to more trouble. He got into several street fights and barroom brawls and spent significant time in the brig. He and a fellow soldier, while stationed in England, were arrested for beating up a couple of Brits. Rocky served twenty-two months in military prison before he was discharged from the Army in 1947.

He came home and went to work for a local coal-and-ice company, using his massive muscles to move piles of materials. He later worked as a ditch-digger and, like his father, toiled for a time in the shoe factory, all the while fighting as an amateur. He knew he did not want to suffer the same fate as his father working for a wealthy factory-owner cashing in on his hard labor, just barely scraping by while spending a lifetime breathing in toxins and chemicals.

So he worked on his physique and his boxing technique. He had a twelve-fight amateur career and won the New England Golden Gloves title before turning pro in 1947 in a fight against Lee Epperson at Valley Arena in Holyoke, Massachusetts. Rocky knocked him out in the third round.

With Allie Colombo by his side, Rocky rose through the ranks and became known as the "Brockton Blockbuster." A buzz built around the young brawler. Hundreds regularly huddled outside the *Brockton Enterprise* building downtown to listen to loudspeakers blaring the radio broadcast of his fights, cheering wildly for Rocky. His father, Pierino, joined those celebrations after his exhausting shift at Adams shoes, beaming proudly about his son.

Everything changed for Rocky and the Marchegianos September 23, 1952, when he beat heavyweight champion Jersey Joe Walcott in thirteen rounds in Philadelphia. That night at Philadelphia Municipal Stadium, Walcott landed a vicious left hook early in the fight that dropped Rocky to the canvas, marking the first time the Brockton brawler had ever been knocked down in a fight. It was a shocking moment for Rocky, but it did not stop him.

In Brockton, a big crowd, which included Pierino, listened anxiously to the broadcast outside the *Enterprise* building. Men in fedoras smoked cigars, shared flasks, and laid their bets with the bookie on the corner as the radio announcer's voice crackled through a bullhorn. Rocky's brothers and sisters listened to the fight at home on a transistor radio, imagining their brother stalking Walcott in the ring before a capacity crowd, a thick haze of Lucky Strike smoke hovering overhead.

The Petronelli brothers were front and center to see their friend make history. They bought five-dollar tickets from a scalper and snuck down to ringside. They watched in awe as Rocky, bleeding profusely from a gash across his nose, mounted an incredible comeback in what was one of the greatest heavyweight title bouts in history.

After Rocky was knocked down, he recovered and settled in for a bruising fight. The class of the heavyweight division at the time, Walcott was ahead on all three scorecards in the thirteenth round when Rocky ended matters. Less than a minute into an uneventful round, Rocky maneuvered Walcott into the ropes and beat him to the punch, landing one of the most famous right hands in history. His soon-to-be-notorious Suzie Q put Walcott on the canvas for good. He was counted out and Rocky was world champion. The Petronellis erupted in celebration, as did the hundreds outside the *Enterprise* listening to the broadcast.

Rocky was crowned the champion. It was an incredible moment for him, the Italian-American community, and the city of Brockton. Rocky returned from Philadelphia and a few days after the fight walked proudly into the Adams shoe factory where his father was hard at work.

"No more shoe-making dad," he told his father.

Tears welled in the older Marchegiano's eyes. They hugged and the young champion escorted his father out of the factory for the last time. It was among the proudest days of Rocky's life.

Rocky gave Walcott a rematch 1953 in Chicago, but it was quick work for The Rock who knocked out the broken ex-champion in the first round. As champion, Rocky built a prodigious undefeated record while trying to avoid being completely sucked into the crooked boxing machine.

He rejected some lucrative offers from Mafia associates to fix fights. The truth is, no Italian-American boxer in the '40s, '50s or '60s, could avoid the grip of the Mafia. Italian boxers in that era had a target on them. Rocky had close ties to many top mobsters—including Providence Mob boss Raymond Patriarca and notorious Murder Inc. triggerman and underworld boxing czar Frankie Carbo, a capo in the Lucchese crime family, and friend to powerful New York mafia don Vito Genovese. Carbo was also a close associate of Rocky's manager, Al Weill, and owned a piece of Rocky. Weill had swindled Rocky out of half his career earnings, which Rocky often cited as a reason for his obsessive penny-pinching. Rocky, in fact, was one of the last people to see Genovese alive when he visited him in a Missouri prison hospital shortly before the mobster died in 1969.

Rocky had a tortured relationship with the Mob. He was, like many Italian fighters of his era, inextricably tied to the criminal underworld, but he refused payoffs to throw fights. And there were consequences. The FBI reported that Rocky received serious threats on his life—and his family's—if he did not take a dive in his September 1954 fight against Ezzard Charles at Yankee Stadium in New York.

Rocky received a letter before the match that read: "We mean business . . . or we will bump off your wife and little child."

Despite the threats, Rocky won a fifteen-round battle with Charles in their first fight on June 17, 1954 at the sold-out Bronx stadium. He won their September 1954 rematch with an eighth-round knockout.

There were, thankfully, no repercussions and there were questions about the seriousness of the threats. Regardless, the whole scenario was common in a dark era for the sport, one in which countless boxers, promoters, bookies, and their associates wound up dead in bars, lakes, Cadillac trunks, and back alleyways.

One of Rocky's closest friends told *Sports Illustrated* in 1993 that he was in a California hotel room with the champ in 1955 when an unnamed mobster tried to convince him to throw his fight against British champ Don Cockell. Cockell was a 10-1 underdog. Rocky could cash in and then reclaim the title in a rematch, the mobster told him.

"Rocky, you can be set the rest of your life if you throw this fight," the gangster told him.

Marciano was furious and ordered the mobster out.

"You disgust me," the fighter told him. "I'm ashamed that you're Italian. Get outta here and don't come back."

Rocky took that anger into the ring in San Francisco. Cockell was 205 pounds and appeared out of shape compared to the 189-pound, solid-as-steel Rocky. Cockell absorbed a tremendous beating as Rocky knocked him through the ropes in the eighth round and knocked him down twice in the ninth before the fight was stopped and Rocky was declared the winner by TKO.

"He's got a lot of guts," Rocky told reporters after the fight of Cockell. "I don't think I ever hit anyone else any more often or harder."

ROCKY, THE MOB, AND A FATEFUL FLIGHT

After winning forty-eight bouts, including forty-two by knockout, Rocky fought his final fight on September 21, 1955, at Yankee Stadium. Rocky was thirty-two. His opponent, Archie Moore, forty-one, was the world light-heavyweight champion and the number-one-ranked heavyweight contender. There were rumors before the fight that it would be Rocky's last.

Rocky's brother, Peter, admits his brother's fire was burning out. Rocky only knew one way to train and that was to put aside all the things in life that he loved—rich foods, good wine, and beautiful women. He trained harder than anyone and was almost always the better conditioned boxer in his fights. It was something he took pride in but his passion was waning. It was also a blueprint in later years for Marvin.

Archie Moore, "The Old Mongoose," analyzed the Cockell fight and gave an infamous interview to *Sports Illustrated* shortly before the September 20, 1955, Yankee Stadium fight.

"Marciano isn't goin' to be any trouble for me," Moore said.

He pointed out Rocky's "stubby" arms and how he missed uppercuts. Moore predicted he would outbox him and take his crown.

"How the man gonna hit me?" Moore asked.

But hit him, Rocky did. It was a tactical fight in the early rounds. Rocky was knocked to the canvas by Moore in the second round, but he recovered quickly. As the rounds accumulated, Rocky punished the older Moore, knocking him down twice in the sixth round and again in the eighth. He sent Moore to the canvas for a fourth time in the ninth round and the challenger could not get up. He was counted out and Rocky had his record forty-ninth victory and forty-third knockout.

After the fight, Rocky was asked if it was his last.

"My mother wants me to retire," Rocky told reporters. "My wife wants me to retire. My whole family wants me to quit. It's been a tough life for them all. I don't know what I will do. I want time to think it over."

The next day, Rocky announced he would fight a fiftieth match, only to reverse course a few months later. On April 27, 1956, he and his manager, Al Weill, held a press conference at the Hotel Shelton in New York City, where Rocky announced his retirement. He said he wanted to spend more time with family but there were also reports he was suffering from nagging injuries, including a bad back.

"No man can say what he will do in the future. But, barring poverty, the ring has seen the last of me," Marciano told reporters. "I am comfortably fixed, and I am not afraid of the future. Barring a complete and dire emergency, you will never see Rocky Marciano make a comeback."

After retiring, Rocky made public appearances and hosted a TV variety show called *The Main Event*, on which he interviewed celebrity guests like Joe DiMaggio and Zsa Zsa Gabor. While he hosted the show and ran around from city to city, his wife, Barbara, was back home waiting for her husband. It wasn't a great marriage, as Rocky would come and go and frequently miss family events. He had become a celebrity—something that most in the humble blue-collar city of Brockton could not understand.

But he did not forget where he came from. In 1956, Goody was training young Navy boxers in Michigan and invited Rocky to be the celebrity referee for the event. Goody knew it would bring some attention and inspiration to the young fighters. Rocky was happy to oblige.

"When Rocky started climbing the ladder to where he was going, he always maintained a good relationship with Goody," Peter Marciano remembers.

Sports was not supposed to be the Petronelli brothers' future. Pat became a union shipbuilder at the Fore River Shipyard in Quincy, Massachusetts, while Goody stayed in the Navy as a medic. They both started training amateur boxers and soon followed in their father's footsteps, setting up their own construction business in Brockton. They hired local kids to work for them, many of whom also worked out at their gyms. Soon, Marvin would be one of them.

Goody and Pat decided to open a gym in Brockton. When Goody told Rocky about the plans, Rocky said he wanted to partner up.

"'How about me going in with you?" he told Goody.

They agreed they would open the gym together once Goody was done with his service. Goody continued serving in the Navy and training boxers, while Rocky traveled the country doing TV interviews, commercials, and making paid appearances. Life on the road affected Rocky's marriage. His wife, Barbara, battled alcohol addiction and they separated for a while. Rocky fathered a son, Rocco, from another woman. Rocky and Barbara worked through their difficulties, rebuilt their relationship, adopted the boy, and raised him together.

Rocky's celebrity life was a whirlwind. By the mid-1960s, he was a household name. He took a part-time gig as a public relations liaison for Raynham-Taunton Greyhound Park, a racetrack a few miles south of Brockton that was among the most profitable in the country. Rocky was friends with Raynham owner George Carney and the track's GM Russ Murray, a former boxer and fight promoter. Rocky took the PR gig to make a few bucks and stay in the public eye while he adjusted to his post-boxing life. He was good at it.

When Sonny Liston fought Muhammad Ali in 1965, Rocky brought Liston and fellow former heavyweight champion Floyd Patterson to Raynham for a meet-and-greet. It made national headlines and brought fans in droves to the track for the rare chance to meet three world heavyweight champions. But more important to management, it brought in thousands to lay bets on the dog races. Rocky hosted other stars at the track, such as Boston Celtics' great K. C. Jones, boxers Willie Pep and "Gentleman" Jim Braddock, and Frank Sinatra.

Rocky had a flair for PR and knew how to make money.

He also earned a reputation as a miser. He always demanded to be paid in cash, often forgoing thousands in payments by check from promoters, managers and others. He had a terrible distrust of the banking system, and especially accountants. He always dealt in cash and sometimes showed up at home with paper bags filled with as much as $40,000. Legend has it that Rocky hid thousands upon thousands in pipes, safety deposit boxes, curtain rods, and wall hides from Brockton to Cuba to Florida to upstate New York to Alaska. None of it has ever been recovered.

As Rocky socialized with the Mob and the Hollywood elite, he pledged to himself to never again be poor. As a personal insurance policy, he started loan-sharking to make extra cash. By 1969, he was said to have had nearly $1 million in loans on the street, including $100,000-plus he loaned to a Mob-connected Cleveland business. There were stories of him collecting debts from deadbeats around Brockton.

His family worried about him. They were especially concerned about his habit of canceling commercial flights so he could keep the cash he was paid in advance for tickets. He would then find small-plane pilots and pay them less to shuttle him around. It was a scheme that nearly cost him his life once before when he survived a crash landing. Despite the brush with death, he did not change his ways.

In 1969, his life was a blur. He was judging beauty pageants and planning to launch a chain of Italian restaurants. His brother, Peter, was going to manage one in California. Rocky also had a construction company, a TV variety show, and even a traveling live show called "Rocky's Knockout Revue," which he brought to hospitals and military bases. He was a regular in the gossip columns from New York to LA.

In February 1969, he and Muhammad Ali met in a Miami TV studio and filmed seventy rounds of simulated boxing that was used in a 1970 film called *The Super Fight* that pitted the two fighters against each other in a computer-simulated title clash. Rocky dropped fifty pounds to prepare for the role and wore a toupee to appear more like his younger self in the film.

The "Super Fight" was the brainchild of a radio producer named Murray Woroner who produced fictional radio broadcasts of heavyweight fights, including greats like Ali, Joe Louis, Jim Braddock, Max Baer, and Gene Tunney. Each fight was simulated using an NCR-315 computer that predicted the outcomes. After one broadcast had Jim Jeffries beating Ali, Ali sued and won a settlement for $10,000. Part of the settlement required Ali and Marciano to participate in the film in exchange for a share of the profits.

That May, Rocky was honored alongside Green Bay Packers icon Vince Lombardi and New York Yankees great Joe DiMaggio at Madison Square Garden by an Italian heritage organization called Americans of Italian Descent. More than twenty thousand people packed the arena, including entertainers Sammy Davis Jr. and Jimmy Durante. That same month, Marciano was in Rome with Brigitte Bardot, Orson Welles, James Garner, Adam West, and other celebrities. He attracted huge crowds and was photographed by the press in front of the Coliseum.

In June 1969, Rocky signed a deal to promote the Attache Phone—the first portable phone with a carrying case. The phone was considered space-age at the time and sold for $2,495. In July, he traveled to a military base in Alaska with fellow former boxing champion Willie Pep for a boxing exhibition. A few days later, he went to Las Vegas and had dinner with Joe Louis. In late July, it was announced that Rocky would star in a pair of Italian films.

On July 31, he refereed amateur bouts in Lawrence, Kansas. A month later, on Monday, August 25, he played golf in an Italian-American Invitational

Tournament in Milwaukee. Rocky was playfully mocked after shooting an unimpressive 87 at Tuckaway Country Club.

"Maybe I don't golf too well," he quipped after the match, "But I'm ready to lick any man in the house."

The next day Rocky traveled to Battle Creek, Michigan, where he spoke and narrated a film about his boxing career for a charity event. On Wednesday, August 27, he participated in a charity powerboat race in Pendleton, Indiana.

He spent two days in the Midwest and on Sunday, August 31, 1969—the night before his forty-seventh birthday—he attended a dinner at the Chicago home of STP oil magnate Andy Granatelli, an Italian immigrant who made a fortune selling synthetic petroleum. Granatelli grew up in the Windy City and was an auto mechanic who promoted car races across the Midwest.

He became a spokesman for STP while he and his brothers built race teams. He and his crew are credited with several auto-racing innovations, including the fully-independent suspension, turbine-powered racecars, and the Novi supercharged V8 engine. Granatelli himself raced cars until a horrific 1948 crash ended his driving career—and nearly his life. His race teams became globally known, and STP became a household name. One of the world's most recognizable and successful drivers, Hall-of-Famer Mario Andretti, was among STP's roster.

Just three months before the dinner with Marciano, Granatelli celebrated his first-ever Indianapolis 500 win when Andretti won for STP. The victory was monumental for Granatelli as his drivers had come close but failed year after year. He was so ecstatic with the win that he ran to the winner's circle and kissed Andretti in what became one of the most iconic photos in auto-racing history. The kiss, though, is viewed by fans of the sport as the beginning of a curse against Andretti and his family. After the photo, Andretti never won another Indy 500, nor did his two sons or any relatives, who had a collective seventy-eight Indy 500 appearances. Many resulted in near-death crashes, mechanical problems, or other catastrophes that gave credence to the "curse of the kiss."

So when Rocky met Granatelli, Granatelli was among the most famous figures in auto racing, his image having skyrocketed after finally winning the Indy 500. STP's brand took off and Granatelli ramped up the marketing. He paid Rocky $5,000 to arm-wrestle with him in a 1969 STP television commercial.

Also with Rocky that final night was Rocky's longtime friend Dominic Santarelli, a Chicago mobster who would be convicted of racketeering in the 1980s. Rocky often spent time with Santarelli in Chicago, including one night in 1965 when The Rock wound up in the city's society pages after partying with Jimmy Durante at a new luxury condo development Santarelli built.

After the two had dinner at Granatelli's mansion, Rocky was to fly to Des Moines, Iowa, to make an appearance at the opening of an insurance agency owned by another shady friend, Frankie Farrell, a businessman who was the son of Des Moines Mob boss Louis Thomas Fratto, also known as "Lew Farrell" or "Cockeyed Louie." Fratto, a close associate of Al Capone, was another former boxer who used the name "Farrell" as a pseudonym.

Fratto ran gambling rackets and was an influential "labor advisor" to the Teamsters and Jimmy Hoffa. He was called "the original Teflon Don" after testifying about the inner workings of the Mafia in three separate congressional hearings into organized crime in the '60s. He was under indictment for extortion in 1967 when he died of cancer at age sixty.

Frankie Farrell was a close associate of Santarelli and, by extension, Rocky. Rocky lived by a strict code of loyalty. If you were his friend, or a close friend of a trusted ally, he would do business with you—for the right price.

Rocky and Farrell were originally supposed to fly from Chicago to Fort Lauderdale so Rocky could attend a birthday party for him and his wife, Barbara, who had turned forty just two days earlier. Also waiting there for him was their daughter, Mary Anne, and their seventeen-month-old adopted son, Rocco, who had just learned to walk. The family was waiting to surprise Rocky by having little Rocco walk to him at the front door carrying presents.

But he made a last-minute decision to postpone the birthday festivities a day so he could fly to Des Moines for the event with Farrell. A nasty storm was moving in, but that did not deter Rocky. Farrell hired pilot Glenn Belz, an inexperienced small-plane pilot with only 231 hours of flying time and no experience flying in foul weather using instruments. Santarelli chose not to go to Des Moines with his friends, a fortuitous decision that haunted him for years.

Granatelli's driver dropped Rocky and Farrell off at Chicago's Midway Airport that afternoon for a 6 p.m. flight. They boarded a Cessna 172 with Belz at the controls. Despite a weather report that included lightning, rain, and winds, the trio took off from Midway, headed for Des Moines.

As the single-engine plane crossed into Newton, Iowa, it lost power and the engine sputtered. Witnesses said they saw it flying just two hundred feet overhead. Around 9 p.m., the plane plummeted downward and struck a tree, shearing off one of its wings. The plane hit the ground, bounced, and slammed into a massive oak tree in an Iowa cornfield, killing all three.

One of the greatest heavyweights of all-time—and an icon in his hometown of Brockton—was dead.

For Goody, it was not only a brutal emotional blow. It doomed their gym.

Or so he thought.

A HERO'S FAREWELL, A NEW JOURNEY BEGINS

No sooner had the Hagler family moved into Brockton than the news broke about Rocky Marciano's death in an Iowa cornfield. Marvin did not know much about Rocky, but he heard people talking about him everywhere he went. The devastating news rocked the city and the boxing world. It was the talk of Brockton in coffee shops, parks, and barrooms and was front-page news for days coast-to-coast.

"This is the saddest news I've ever heard," Joe Louis told the Associated Press.

While the Haglers settled into their new home, Rocky's remains were transported back to Boston's Logan International Airport and then to Hickey Funeral Home in Brockton. Rocky's death was so shocking and impacted so many people that two memorial services were held. The first was in Brockton where three thousand mourners—including US Senator Ted Kennedy, several boxing champions, and dozens of elected officials and military leaders—packed Saint Colman Catholic Church, where Rocky and his wife got married.

Following the Brockton service, the boxer's flag-draped coffin was flown to Florida where another massive wake attracted many celebrities, including Muhammad Ali and Joe Louis, who attended together. A journalist approached the two men and asked for their thoughts on Rocky.

"We'll do this any time, we'll talk about Rocky whenever you want, but not now," Ali told the reporter. "We're here to honor not only a great, great fighter but a great man."

At St. Pius Church in Fort Lauderdale, Louis gave a stirring eulogy.

"It seems such a shame to us that God would take away such a fine man," Louis said. "But as far as everyone in the world of boxing is concerned, God got the best when he took away Rocky Marciano."

The only undefeated heavyweight champion in boxing history was laid to rest in Queen of Haven Cemetery in Fort Lauderdale. Back in Brockton, the city mourned Marciano as its brightest star was gone. No one in the Shoe City knew who Marvin Hagler was at that moment, but there was another young Italian fighter at the Petronelli gym who was starting to make a name for himself: Pat Petronelli's son, Tony.

Born in nearby East Bridgewater, Tony was one of the best boxers in Brockton in the early '70s when Marvin moved to the city. A tough, fast-handed super lightweight, Tony labored for his father's construction company during the day and trained at night.

He was getting noticed on the New England fight circuit. Just seventeen years old in 1970, he built a 13-1 amateur record with ten knockouts. His only loss came in the New England Golden Gloves—the Northeast's premier amateur tournament—when he lost in the semifinals. Tony climbed the amateur ranks and was on his way to becoming a pro. He was not Rocky Marciano, but for Pat and Goody, the wiry young fighter was a welcome project to focus on while they grieved the loss of their friend Rocky and tried to rebuild their boxing future.

It was clear Tony was going to be a good pro boxer, but the brothers did not know if he had the ability and power to become a world champion. He trained hard, was dedicated, and was a great leader in the gym. The younger kids looked up to Tony and knew that he was on his way to becoming a professional. He was tough, quick, and could slip punches. But they could not pin their hopes on Pat's boy just yet.

For Goody and Pat, training fighters was their passion, but their construction company paid the bills. It was starting to look more and more like Goody and Pat's fight-game dreams died with Rocky in that Iowa cornfield.

While the brothers tried to figure out a way forward without Rocky, Brockton too was struggling to reinvent itself as the shoe industry collapsed. Most of the factories had closed and jobs were scarce. Only a few shoe companies remained, including Etonic and Foot Joy, which had become premier golf-shoe brands that still made many of their signature leather shoes in the city.

There was still one major employer: office-supply giant W. B. Mason, which had been in Brockton since 1898. W. B. Mason, which is today still headquartered in Brockton, was founded as a manufacturer of rubber stamps and engraved products. As the shoe industry exploded, W. B. expanded into office supplies. The company grew rapidly and became one of the nation's largest office suppliers as they stocked the local shoe companies with furniture, paper, pencils, pens, ink, boxes, and other products. While a few hundred jobs remained at W. B., the exodus of the shoe industry was taking its toll on the city.

Like many post-industrial American cities, Brockton was faced with trying to figure out how to repurpose suddenly-vacated massive factories. Urban blight took hold as poverty, crime, and despair spread. Yet Ida Mae never questioned whether it was safer than Newark. She had no reason to go back to New Jersey. She had family and a growing network of neighbors and friends to help her out in Brockton.

She had her hands full raising six kids. Aunt Cat's apartment on North Main Street quickly got too crowded so Ida Mae moved her family to a three-bedroom apartment on Summer Street, across from the Crescent Court public housing project. Marvin started hanging out at Crescent Court when he was not working.

"He got along with everybody," Artie Dias, a childhood friend of Marvin, said. "He didn't have any problems with anyone. Everybody got along with everybody back then."

Dias was a percussionist in a local funk band called Mr. T and the Troublemen, which they later changed to Mr. T and the BC Five. BC stood for "Brockton Children." The band played house parties in the Crescent Court projects, doing covers of classic '60s and '70s funk bands such as The O'Jays, Ohio Players, Kool & the Gang, and Earth, Wind & Fire. They were managed by their mothers and got a few gigs at local bars, including one called The Underground, which was located on Centre Street next to the Petronelli Brothers' gym.

Marvin loved music and came to many of the BC Five's gigs. Sometimes, Artie and the band would let him tag along, so long as he helped carry their gear. Some of Ida Mae's other kids were not adjusting quite as well as Marvin. Veronica started hanging out late at night and sometimes ran with a rough crowd. Drinking and smoking weed was common in the projects among the teenagers. Marvin was often the one who had to check on her to make sure she was safe and was not getting into trouble.

Cheryl, meanwhile, was traumatized by the move to Brockton. She was depressed about leaving her friends back in Newark. Her emotional distress was so profound that she stopped talking completely. The schools put her in speech therapy.

"She brings me to this place with all these people that I don't know, besides the family. I just shut down," Cheryl recalls. "I just stopped talking."

Marvin helped her, as he did all his younger siblings.

"He was very caring," she says. "He wasn't afraid. He wasn't scared of anything. He was a great help to my mother for all of us."

Marvin kept hearing about Rocky and started to realize Brockton was a great fighting city. He started to get curious, but he had only dabbled in boxing back in Newark in sandlots with Mr. Joe. He had never sparred or done a proper boxing workout.

His laborer's job had him in tip-top shape and he became obsessed with working out. His uncles, Brother and Buddy, were both in great shape.

Uncle Brother had spent many years incarcerated and was in "prison shape," Cheryl recalls.

"Marvin looked up to our uncles and wanted to be in-shape like them," she says.

Marvin started buying bodybuilding magazines and did the workouts in the diagrams in the glossy pages. He'd get home at night after working all day and hit the living-room floor, obsessively working out and imitating the exercises in the magazine.

He was a sixteen-year-old high school dropout in a new city with few friends. It was not long before he started getting in fights on the street.

One night, fate intervened in the form of a rival named Dornell Wigfall.

STREET FIGHTING MAN

Dornell Wigfall was a well-known tough guy and standout athlete. He wore number 82 on the Brockton High School Boxers football team—a team that took its nickname from Rocky Marciano. The football coach was Armond Colombo, an Italian American from in Brockton. He was also Rocky's brother-in-law, as well as the brother of Rocky's friend and trainer, the late Allie Colombo. A 1949 graduate of Brockton High, Armond married Rocky's sister Betty in 1959.

In 1969, Colombo was in just his second year of coaching Brockton High. His first season was not great as the team went a disappointing 3-6. But the city rallied around the reeling Marciano and Colombo families after the deaths of Allie and Rocky. Brockton officials named the new stadium at Brockton High "Marciano Stadium" that year. It was a state-of-the-art high school stadium with seating for ten thousand people—the largest schoolboy stadium in Massachusetts at the time.

It was a huge responsibility thrust upon Colombo as the city christened the new facilities. He was faced with a tall task, not only to turn around the school's football program after a dismal season, but also to honor his brother-in-law Rocky. He did not take the responsibility lightly. Colombo vowed to go undefeated as a tribute to his brother-in-law and friend.

Dornell Wigfall was a key piece of Colombo's plan. He was a magnificent athlete, a defensive stalwart on that Boxers squad, and did his part to make his coach's dream come true.

The Boxers blitzed through their schedule, crushing school after school. Wigfall racked up sacks, fumble recoveries and tackles while his teammate, future Notre Dame and San Francisco 49ers star tight end Ken MacAfee, racked up touchdowns. They went 9-0 and won the school's first of what would be many high school Super Bowls under Colombo.

That season was the turning point for a program that dominated Massachusetts football for decades. Wigfall embedded himself in the winning culture Colombo created. After that undefeated Super Bowl season, the college offers poured in for Wigfall. Every school wanted him. The New England Patriots came to Marciano Stadium to scout MacAfee, a six-foot-four-inch, 250-pound stud, but they came away more impressed by Wigfall.

But like too many Brockton kids, the lure of the streets and fast money proved to be too much. Colombo was planning to play him the following season as a two-way player, adding halfback to his defensive duties, but Wigfall punched a cop and went to jail, ending not only his football career, but also his education. He dropped out of school and started boxing, while dabbling in crime.

Wigfall lived in Crescent Court, just across the street from the Ward 5 Gym which was attached to a bar run by Gigi Sergio, a stocky, tough businessman who ran rackets and was an associate of the Patriarca crime family in nearby Providence. Wiseguys came and went through the smoky barroom, meeting with Gigi, checking out the local boxers, running numbers, and plotting how to loan-shark and collect from deadbeats.

Gigi was a regular at the Raynham-Taunton Greyhound Park, which at the time was one of the most profitable racetracks in the country. Owner George Carney, who grew up with Rocky, Goody, and Pat, also grew up with Gigi and recalled how he held court at the track with Vecchione and others from the Ward 5 club—and beyond. Carney recalled Gigi as a "good guy," but said he had to keep his distance because Carney was licensed by the Massachusetts Gaming Commission and it was common knowledge that Gigi was involved with the Mafia.

"I couldn't socialize with him because his business and my business were two different sides of the street," Carney said.

Dornell Wigfall, however, was attracted to the fast life and the money. With no sports or school in his life, he started hanging out at the bar and became one of Gigi's henchmen, chasing down deadbeats and making them pay.

Gigi was born in Brockton to Italian immigrant parents. He joined the United States Navy and served in Korea before returning home and setting up shop at the Ward 5. The club later was renamed Gigi's Lounge, a scrappy blue-collar bar that still stands today. The wood-paneled, billiard-table strewn barroom embodies the cliché *If these walls could talk*. Many of those stories would involve Wigfall.

When the Ward 5 first opened, Gigi let any neighborhood kid who strolled into the club lace them up in the backroom boxing gym. Countless young Brockton kids in the early '70s cut their way through the smoky pub for a shot at ring glory. Or at least a chance to escape the doldrums and dangers of day-to-day project life.

Wigfall was one of them. When Marvin arrived in Brockton, Wigfall was already fighting amateur. Marvin found out pretty quickly the vast difference between a semi-tough guy and a trained fighter one night in the Crescent Court projects. Marvin liked to have a good time, so he often did what all teenagers do—he found a local house party. He was cocky, had a chip on his shoulder, liked a drink or two, and loved the ladies.

Unfortunately for Marvin, one of the girls he decided to chat up at the party was with Dornell. Victoria Hagler, Marvin's sister, was having a drink and hanging out with her friends when she saw her brother try to dance with a girl. Wigfall, towering over the party, moved right in.

"That's my woman," he said to Marvin.

"Uh-oh, here we go," Veronica said to herself.

Despite giving up six inches, Marvin did not back down. Marvin had an angry streak and a reckless side and was not afraid to fight. After all, he had just escaped some of the worst rioting the nation had ever seen. What was some punk in a Brockton apartment to him?

"He had everyone scared of him," Hagler said. "But he didn't scare me. Coming from New Jersey like I did, if I didn't get you one way, I got you another. I hit you in the head with a bottle, or a brick. But I'll gitcha!"

But Veronica knew her brother was in trouble. She knew all about Wigfall. Everyone did.

"Marvin, don't fight this guy; you know he's a fighter. He's conditioned," she told her brother.

Marvin did not listen. So they went outside, followed by sixty or so teenagers. As Marvin went to remove his leather bomber jacket, Wigfall pounced, pummeling him ruthlessly with lefts and rights—the blows of a trained fighter exploding on young Marvin's not-yet-battle-tested face. Marvin took a brutal shot to the jaw. He was in trouble. He fell to the ground and rolled away from Wigfall's flurry, taking cover under a car.

Wigfall's brother Charles was riding his bike down the street toward the party when he saw his brother standing by the car, shouting at Marvin to come out from underneath. Charles and Marvin were friends who hung out regularly, having drinks and running the streets of the East Side.

"Dornell never bullied anybody, but he could take care of himself very well," Charles Wigfall said. "I saw Dornell had Marvin underneath the car. You know, Marvin womanized on the wrong woman. That was Dornell. Man, I'll tell you, when I saw that I couldn't believe it. Cause we were all friends."

Wigfall was satisfied with the beating and the message it sent to Marvin or anyone else who wondered if Wigfall was the real deal. Veronica ran to her brother, helped him out from under the car and they went to the hospital. Marvin had a bruised jaw and cracked tooth but otherwise was OK.

He knew he was beaten by a trained fighter, but he was still angry. He wanted revenge. He would get it, but it would take time. Years in fact.

"SO YOU WANNA BOX, KID?"

Marvin walked up the old wooden staircase to the Petronelli Brothers gym on Centre Street, each dusty step creaking under the weight of his chiseled teenage frame. The walls were adorned with yellowing black-and-white photos and frayed boxing posters of Rocky.

Some photos showed Rocky being paraded past thousands of fans on the streets just outside the building. Men in boxy, pin-striped suits, fedoras, and bowler hats cheered alongside women in 1940s-style swing dresses as the city celebrated Rocky's title defenses over some of the greatest boxers in history. Marvin was in the champ's church. It was sacred ground.

Everyone he met seemed to talk about the Brockton Blockbuster and how much he meant to the city. Marvin listened and took note, especially to the tales of how Rocky outworked everyone he fought. Marvin was fascinated with the old timers' stories of Rocky's hardcore training regimen, his relentless focus, and total commitment to being the top conditioned athlete in the ring at every one of his fights. It was a lesson that stuck with Marvin his entire career.

Still stinging from the Wigfall beating, Marvin sat solemnly on a bench in the Petronelli gym in cutoff jeans, steely-eyed, watching the boxers train.

He listened to the machine gun thwap of the speed bags, the low pulses of the heavy bags, the rapid cracks of the jump ropes, and the grunts and snorts of the fighters working out. He took in the smells: a mixture of dust, sweat, leather, aged oak flooring, and floor polish. He had ventured into Vinnie Vechionne's gym a few days earlier but was ignored. It was an oversight Gigi and Vecchione never got over.

Like Goody and Pat, Marvin was looking for his future. He was angry at the world and angry about being beat up by Wigfall at Crescent Court.

"I didn't trust anybody," Marvin later said.

He also felt "out of place" because he had moved from "an all-Black society to a mixed society."

"The only place I'd run across whites was in stores. They were always behind the counters, taking the cash. School principals. Police. The post office. I really didn't trust them," Hagler told *Sports Illustrated* writer William Nack in 1982. "If they were nice, I thought, 'What do they want from me?' I had to learn for myself how people really were. When I found out all white people weren't bad, I started to relax around them. It took me a long time. Goody and Pat had a lot to do with that."

Goody and Pat wanted to build on the legend of Rocky and find the next great champion. Little did they know that champion had just walked in.

Goody noticed the new kid sitting alone on a wooden bench, watching intently. The bell rang signaling the end of a round for the boxers working out. The bell was the start of a one-minute break for the fighters at their various stations—the heavy bag, shadowboxing, sparring, jumping rope, doing sit-ups. Goody walked over to Marvin. He stopped in front of him and Marvin looked up at the grizzled trainer.

"Do you want to learn how to fight?" Goody asked him.

"That's what I'm here for," Marvin replied.

"You ever fight before?" Goody responded.

"A little," Marvin said. "Really just in the streets."

"What's your name kid?" the trainer asked.

"Marvin Hagler, sir," he replied.

"OK Marvin Hagler. Let's go."

Goody grabbed him some old, beat-up gloves and worked him out. It was quickly apparent he had talent and raw skill, punching power, a rare toughness, and most of all, an edge. He was naturally right-handed. Goody showed him some moves, how to slip punches, and taught him some basic footwork, before sending the young man on his way.

"Come on back kid," Goody told him.

Marvin nodded and walked out alone.

It was a routine interaction for Goody. Countless young kids found their way into the gym day after day. Some would work out for a day or two; others for a week or a month before losing interest. Goody was not sure at that moment if Marvin was interested, never mind great, but there was one thing he was sure of: the kid had intensity. There was something unique about him.

Marvin went home that night and stood in front of the mirror working on the moves Goody showed him—over and over. He went back to the gym the next day and worked out with Goody again. To the trainer's surprise, the kid repeated the moves perfectly. That, Goody remembered, was not normal.

"You look good," Goody told him.

"I've been practicing, looking in the mirror at home in my bedroom at different punches, different combinations," Marvin told him.

There were a lot of fighters at Petronelli Brothers Gym then, including Tony Petronelli. Goody was impressed by the new kid and started working with him every day. Soon, he'd be sparring with Tony.

"I started teaching him and I liked what I saw," Goody later recalled. "He was very dedicated. He listened. He was serious."

Soon Marvin was working for the brothers' construction company, lugging around cement, sand, and rocks, piling up cinder blocks and sweeping up jobsites. He worked alongside Tony many days. Tony's career was just starting to take off. After work, they went to the gym together and Marvin carried Tony's gear up the flight of stairs. When Tony started having fights at Brockton High and in Taunton, New Bedford, and Providence, Marvin was allowed to tag along, but he had to carry Tony's gear.

Marvin did not mind. He was fascinated with this new world. And it would not be long before the roles were reversed. Marvin was starting to trust the Petronelli Brothers, and Tony, who at the time were the only white people in his life.

After working out, Marvin would often walk home through the streets of downtown Brockton alone. Rocky had given Brockton quiet, tough leadership, inspiration, and tremendous civic pride. Marvin became captivated by his legend and the city's boxing culture and wanted to be part of it. His goal became to be the city's next great prizefighter. Just like Rocky.

"In Newark I'd never heard of Rocky Marciano," Marvin told the *New York Times* in 1983. "But as soon as I hit Brockton, I found out.... From what everybody told me, he always kept himself in very good condition. He was from the old school."

Marvin was just fifteen but the Petronellis knew they had a talent on their hands and started lining up amateur fights for him. He lied about his age to get into amateur tournaments, using a fake birth certificate that said he was born in 1952 rather than 1954. At five-feet-nine-inches, he was shorter than most of the fighters his weight. The brothers affectionately called him "Short Stuff," which soon was shortened to just "Stuff."

"What I saw at first was this thing about whitey and this tendency to talk big like a lot of the kids," Goody recalled of his first impressions of Marvin in those early days at the gym. "What separated him was his patience and drive, his dedication. . . . He had a heart as big as Brockton."

Marvin may have been just a lost kid, but he fell in love with the sport and the gym. He slowly began to trust that the Petronelli brothers were different from the other whites he had come across in his life and realized he had found something special. He obsessively practiced the techniques Goody taught him and developed a passion for boxing. He saw boxing as an opportunity. He was fascinated by Goody's teachings. Goody quickly found Marvin had not only great discipline, but a unique killer instinct as well.

"I have a real love for the moves, the strategies," Marvin recalled. "I like the feels and the smells. I like the colors. I remember putting on my first pair of red gloves and saying they were red because that was the color of blood."

Marvin spent his days earning three dollars an hour digging ditches, pouring concrete, and framing buildings around Brockton. His work ethic and discipline impressed the military-trained Petronelli Brothers. Whatever the task—hitting the heavy bag for an hour, skipping rope, sparring bigger opponents, hauling cement up rickety stairs, shoveling hundreds of pounds of sand and dirt—he focused and got it done.

Goody and Pat built trust with him slowly. They would take him out to lunch and he'd try to chip in with a dollar or two because he did not want to owe them anything. But Pat and Goody would assure him it was their treat. It took a while before Marvin accepted their generosity.

"Goody and Pat amazed me," Marvin said. "We'd go out to lunch and they'd say 'Keep your dollar. This is on us.' I'd think they were going to take it out of my paycheck at the end of the week. But they didn't. They said, 'Marvin, when you make it big you can pay us back.'"

In the ring, Marvin was an immediate winner. After winning one of his early amateur bouts, he made a stunning comment to Goody.

"I'm going to be world champion," Marvin proclaimed.

Goody had seen this youthful bravado many times before. A lot of young fighters talk big. But then life gets in the way. They got jobs, girlfriends, wives and kids, and boxing became a hobby. Or they quit altogether.

"Sure you will, kid," Goody replied. "And I'll be your coach."

MARVIN AND BERTHA

While Marvin immersed himself in the sport and spent his nights at the Petronelli Brothers' gym, Ida Mae was not sure that her son would truly become a fighter.

"He always said he wanted to be a boxer," she told *Sports Illustrated*. "I didn't believe him when he said he wanted to be like Floyd Patterson. I thought he'd become a social worker."

He was deadly serious. In his locker at the gym, he hung a picture of himself and signed it "Future Champion of the World."

"He had those eyes that look right through you," Goody said. "I remember him taking me in the back room and telling me he was born to be a champion."

He fought constantly—sometimes two or three times in a week—and built an impressive amateur record, knocking out most everyone he faced. None of them worked out like Marvin. None of them had the drive he had. None of them wanted to put in the work to be a champion like he did. And none of them had the Petronelli brothers in their corner.

When he was twelve or thirteen in Newark, Marvin met a young woman named Bertha Washington, who lived with her family in Brockton. Her parents were friends with Ida Mae and they came to Newark to visit over Thanksgiving. Marvin and Bertha hit it off and became friends but lost touch when she went back to Brockton.

When Ida Mae and the family moved to Brockton, Bertha was one of the few kids he knew besides some cousins. He and Bertha reconnected and started hanging out around Brockton's East Side. She said Marvin was "shy" but was handsome and had lots of girls around him in those early days. He wore his hair in a tight afro, in the style of the times, and was somewhat cocky. At first, they were friends, but she said they actually considered themselves "cousins" because they were so close.

Bertha was a year older than Marvin. She had her first son, Jimmy (also known as "Pee-wee"), and married her first husband in 1971 when she was eighteen. She had a second child, a daughter named Celeste, two years later. While Marvin was getting used to Brockton and starting his fight career, she was raising her babies. They would hang out sometimes, but it was not love at first sight. It would take some time before they would become close.

"I couldn't stand him and he couldn't stand me," she told the *Boston Globe* in 1981 of their early days in Brockton. "I thought he was too conceited . . . he was always in front of the mirror."

With two kids and just barely twenty, Bertha soon separated from her first husband. She and Marvin started dating and he moved into an apartment with Bertha and her two kids. Ida Mae, meanwhile, moved the family to Southfield Gardens, a neighborhood on Brockton's South Side.

Marvin still helped his mother, but suddenly he was running his own household and helping Bertha raise her kids. He continued to work during the day and hit the gym at night. To say the brothers knew he had the chance to be a champion would be a stretch, but it was clear to them he was worth their time and investment.

"His passion for boxing was intense," Goody later recalled. "He appeared fascinated with boxing and seemed to love everything about it from the smell of the liniment and the rich leather of the boxing gloves through to the different techniques he saw the other boxers practicing."

Personally, the brothers took it slow with Marvin. They knew about his background coming from Newark and that he was not comfortable around white people, especially those in positions of authority. But Marvin certainly was not the first jaded young Black man to walk into their gym. They were truly from the old school—World War II vets. They had served alongside many young men like Marvin who came from tough upbringings. They believed that if they gave him opportunity, challenged him, taught him proper technique, and showed him that they cared about him, he would respond positively.

"I recognized that it would take time to cement and mature a trust and friendship with him," Goody said. "Marvin seemed to have a deep distrust about white people and so I took my time."

They hoped his anger and mistrust would drive him, which happened. Marvin beat everyone sent his way as an amateur. He developed knockout power and an edge. He also had a strong chin. As he accumulated victories, Goody and Pat spent more and more time working with Marvin. They focused on helping him develop a signature punch, much like Rocky had with his "Suzie Q" overhand right.

"He developed a good straight left hand," Goody said.

In May 1973, just before his nineteenth birthday, Marvin fought in the National Amateur Athletic Union tournament at the Hynes Convention Center in Boston. There was buzz about this young southpaw from Brockton via Newark who was knocking out all comers.

His performance at the Hynes had the Northeast boxing crowd sitting up and taking notice. Among them was "Suitcase" Sam Silverman, a legendary New England fight promoter who earned his nickname because he was said to always have a suitcase stuffed with cash in the trunk of his car. Silverman, who worked with the Petronelli brothers and promoted some of their fighters, said of Hagler: "This kid has the best shot of any kid in New England of winning a national title."

The media too was starting to take notice. It was late, great *Boston Globe* columnist Will McDonough who wrote the very first news story about Marvin. McDonough grew up the youngest of nine in an Irish-Catholic home in South Boston and started as a copy boy at the *Globe* in 1955, covering schoolboy sports and amateur boxing. He went on to become the *Globe*'s top sportswriter and one of the top pro football writers and sports TV personalities in America.

McDonough was a *Globe* staffer in 1973 and covered the tournament at the Hynes, where Marvin scored a first-round TKO over McArthur Freeman of Georgia. Marvin rocked Freeman with a shot to the jaw in the first minute of the fight. Thirty seconds later, another shot launched a near-legless Freeman into the ropes and the fight was stopped. Freeman never fought again.

"I've been in my hotel room fighting myself in the mirror for two days and it was getting me mad," he told McDonough. "I wanted to take it out on someone."

McDonough was an ace reporter and was there looking for a scoop about an up-and-coming fighter. He saw something special in the young boxer from Brockton that night and profiled him in the *Globe*. It was a prescient decision by McDonough as that first interview provided early insight into Marvin, his work ethic, and his relationship with the Petronelli brothers. McDonough's piece also gave the first signs of the growing bond between Goody and Marvin.

"I took the week off and I'm not getting paid, but I don't mind because my boss is a good guy," the young fighter told McDonough, referring to Goody.

Marvin also gave a glimpse of the killer instinct he would soon become famous—or infamous—for, telling McDonough about the Freeman fight: "I didn't want it to stop. I wanted to knock him out *for good*."

For an amateur, those were bold, perhaps even shocking, comments. His words were not playful, Ali-esque bravado. They were not said with a smile. They were the words of an angry, driven young man.

McDonough's piece was the first to capture Marvin's complex persona, which often vacillated between vulnerability and braggadocio. It was a yin-and-yang dynamic that would define Marvin throughout his life and career.

Some close to him say his bravado was a defense mechanism. While he knew he was good, perhaps even great, he was somewhat insecure. Bragging like Ali or other sports superstars was what he thought he was supposed to do to project strength. So at times he did just that, and gave the media what he thought they wanted to hear.

"That was the first big tournament I was ever in and I was nervous," he told McDonough, before adding, with confidence, "I'm going all the way. I'm in great shape. I feel really strong."

Despite making brazen statements at times, Marvin's tough talk was not totally natural for him. Deep down, he was humble, even fearful. Fearful he would not reach his potential. Fearful he would fail and become mired in a life of poverty.

Just like Rocky.

After defeating McArthur Freeman, Marvin was pitted in the semifinals against World Military Champion and the previous year's National AAU runner-up Russ Fickling, a rugged southpaw and US Navy serviceman. Fickling too had destroyed his first opponent in the tournament.

Marvin won a unanimous three-round decision over Fickling and went on to pummel Atlanta-born US Marine Terry Dobbs in the finals.

"He looked like old Henry Armstrong," Goody said after the Dobbs fight, comparing Marvin to the Golden Age all-time great. "He had everything that night: heart, desire. Dobbs was a big, tall guy and Marvin stood on him until he dropped. He really showed me something."

Marvin was beaming after the victory, but as he was trained to do by Goody and Pat, he contained his excitement. They all knew he had beaten a very good fighter but there were many others out there waiting for him who were much better. He had a lot to learn.

"He had that desire," Goody said. "He'd get a little swollen lip or a black eye and he'd come back the next day. Those are the kids you look for. But you don't promise 'em nothin'."

It was around this time that Marvin's iconic nickname was given to him. One story says that the name was given to him by a Lowell boxing writer who described young Marvin's showboating theatrics and compared him to Ali. But in truth, it came from a ring announcer at the Golden Gloves tournament in Dartmouth, Massachusetts, a small town next to New Bedford. The Golden Gloves matches were held at the Lincoln Park Ballroom, a smoke-filled venue on the grounds of a classic New England amusement park.

Hagler fought there many nights after the roller coaster had shut down for the evening and gave thrilling and bloody beatings to fellow teenagers and young men from across New England. It was not long before trainers started trying to duck the Petronellis, fearful of putting their fighters in the ring with Marvin. The kid was a southpaw and a killer—the kind of fighter that ended careers.

The Golden Gloves promoters often had to horse-trade with trainers to get Marvin opponents. Lenny "Low Price" Kaplan, a businessman from Fall River with a deep, gravelly voice, was the public address announcer at Lincoln Park for decades. He often gave the teenaged fighters nicknames to hype up the crowd. One night, after Marvin knocked out some kid in fifty seconds, Kaplan announced him as "Marvelous Marvin."

The nickname stuck, so much so that Marvin legally changed his name to Marvelous years later. Hagler thanked Kaplan in 1981 for coming up with his ring name. In 1973, following one of his last amateur bouts, Marvin made another bold prediction to longtime Golden Gloves promoter Joe Morrissette.

"I don't have a nickel to my name, but I will be the world champion middleweight," Marvin said.

SUITCASE SAM

Marvin won forty of his fifty-two amateur bouts and was the best young middleweight in New England by the end of 1973. There was buzz that he would join Team USA for the 1976 Olympic Games in Montreal. But Marvin had other ideas.

He was broke, helping Bertha raise the kids, helping his mother raise his brother and sisters and needed to earn money. So waiting three years to go fight for a medal was not an option.

"I'll never get to the Olympics," Marvin said. "I'm working as a machine apprentice and am too old."

Marvin could not wait any longer. He needed income, so he turned pro.

"You can't take a trophy and turn it in for a bagful of groceries," he later said of abandoning an Olympic bid.

Goody and Pat turned to their friend Suitcase Sam. A partner of fellow boxing legends Rip Valenti and Johnny Buckley, Silverman was a colorful character who stood out in a sport chock-full of them. The Boston promoter started matchmaking in the 1930s, orchestrated some of the first televised bouts, and was the king of New England boxing for decades. He made a name for himself promoting thirty-two of Rocky Marciano's fights.

He was also a PR genius who once set up a ring in a downtown Boston department-store window for Sugar Ray Robinson to train for his fight against Paul Pender. Shoppers came by to watch Sugar Ray train and dropped money into a jar that was said to go to charity. Silverman held the weigh-in right there in the store window.

He was tough and brazen. He was known to slip cash-stuffed envelopes to reporters to get good press for himself and his fighters. He also cavorted with organized crime figures, was married to an ex-showgirl, and had a criminal rap sheet.

He was once slugged in the jaw in a restaurant near Boston Garden by a thug wearing brass knuckles. He survived two assassination attempts. In 1951, someone fired bullets through his house in Chelsea, a city next to Boston, one of which nearly struck his wife. Another time, four bombs blew up at his house, but luckily neither he nor anyone was home. The failed attacks were said to be the work of New York gangsters seeking to muscle in on his TV deals and take a piece of his New England boxing fiefdom.

In 1965, Silverman saw one of the biggest scores of his life slip through his hands. He was the initial promoter for the rematch between Muhammad Ali and Sonny Liston. The heavyweights' first fight a year earlier in Miami ended in controversy as Liston quit in the seventh round. There were allegations of a fix, while Liston claimed he injured his shoulder and could not go on.

An immediate rematch was announced just as Ali joined the Nation of Islam, which to white America and the press in those days was the same as announcing you were a terrorist. Liston, meanwhile, returned home to Denver, where he was busted for drunk driving in his Cadillac with a loaded handgun. Liston had dozens of previous arrests and had been grilled a few years earlier in a congressional investigation into organized crime and corruption in boxing. He was not America's sweetheart.

Neither was Ali, so several states refused to sanction the fight. Silverman, though, was able to persuade the Massachusetts Boxing Commission to give him a license and the rematch was scheduled for November 16, 1964, at Boston Garden. Three days before the fight, however, on Friday the 13th, Ali suffered a hernia and the fight was delayed for six months.

During the delay, Liston was arrested two more times. More concerns arose over possible organized crime involvement and fight-fixing in the first match, prompting Boston's District Attorney to step in and block the fight. It was a huge blow to Silverman as the fight would have elevated him to national status in the sport.

Instead, the rematch was moved to a hockey arena in Lewiston, Maine, where Ali stopped Liston in the first round, scoring one of the most controversial knockouts in history. Liston went down after a flicking right hand from Ali, but many observers believe that the blow never connected and accused Liston of taking a dive. It has been theorized that Liston either was paid by mobsters to throw the fight or that he caved to threats from the Nation of Islam. Although the fight became infamous for the "phantom punch," investigations into its outcome were inconclusive.

For Silverman, it was always the big one that got away. Three years later, in 1968, he was arrested by FBI agents and charged with fight-fixing, but the case was dismissed just days before trial.

Despite the scandals, Goody and Pat continued to work with Suitcase Sam. After all, he had contacts that they did not. They knew him from Silverman's days working with Rocky and built a good relationship with him as he booked fights for their fighters, including Pat's son, Tony. They approached him, told him about their new hard-punching southpaw, and Silverman agreed to set up Marvin's first pro bout.

It was scheduled for the Brockton High School gym and paid Marvin just fifty dollars. The massive school, which opened in 1970, housed five thousand students and had a beautiful new gym where a ring was set up with seats for several hundred fans.

Silverman paired Marvin with Terry Ryan, from Richmond, Virginia. Before the fight, Silverman told Goody to have Marvin fight right-handed so he would be faster. Marvin did as instructed and knocked Ryan out in the second round of a scheduled four-rounder for his first professional win.

Tony Petronelli fought in the main event. Tony was 13-1 at the time with ten knockouts and won a ten-round decision against John "Flash" Howard, also from Richmond. It was a good night for Goody and Pat.

But Suitcase Sam was not impressed. After the fight, Silverman told Goody to switch Marvin back to southpaw.

"Turn him back lefthanded," Silverman told Goody. "He's more dynamic that way."

"Sam, make up your mind," Goody told the promoter.

Goody did what he was told but Marvin did not completely listen. From that day forward, Marvin fought as a southpaw, but was in fact a switch-hitter who changed to orthodox as he saw fit. In his second bout, he won a six-round decision over Sonny Williams in Boston on July 25, 1973. Two weeks later, he scored a second-round KO over Muhammad Smith for his third victory.

His chin was stone, his conditioning impeccable, and his recovery time superhuman. He did not get hit much so he could bounce back quickly to get back into the ring for the next payday, small as they were. Boxing was becoming a good supplemental income source for Hagler and he was starting to see that he could make a living with his fists.

As Marvin kept winning, he continued working for the brothers' construction company and trained harder and harder. Goody saw not only glimpses of greatness from his new protege, he started seeing an uncanny resemblance to Rocky.

"He doesn't have Rocky's style. Rocky's defense was his offense," Goody recalled. "But Marvin's got the same heart Rocky had. Marvin kept telling us that he was going to be a champion someday."

Marvin's nemesis Dornell Wigfall, meanwhile, continued to fight at the Ward 5. Jack Cashin, who grew up on the East Side and sparred with Wigfall, remembered him as "a great athlete."

"He was a great fighter," Cashin recalled. "He was long and lean and rangy."

Wigfall made his pro debut on March 14, 1973, against another first-time pro, Vincent Perry. The fight was at Roseland Ballroom in Taunton, Massachusetts, another hardscrabble industrial city of fifty thousand people, located about fifteen minutes south of Brockton. While Brockton was famous for its shoe factories, Taunton was known as the Silver City because it was home to Reed & Barton, one of the top silversmith companies in America at the time. The company made expensive silverware, trophies, and gifts, employed thousands in the region and even manufactured medals for the Olympics.

Roseland was a gem in the city, just down the street from Reed & Barton. It was a gorgeous, one-thousand-person-capacity ballroom and nightclub. A cavernous venue with ornate décor, Roseland hosted fights, shows, and concerts. In the 1930s and '40s, it was an essential stop on the Big Band circuit of the era, hosting Benny Goodman, Tommy Dorsey, Louis Armstrong, Ella Fitzgerald, Glenn Miller, and Frank Sinatra.

In fact, Sinatra was so enchanted with Roseland that he had his own private box, where he was known to entertain his La Cosa Nostra friends, including Providence Mob boss Raymond Patriarca. Sinatra and his Rat Pack partner Dean Martin spent a lot of time in Massachusetts, often socializing with organized crime figures. The duo were part-owners of the former Berkshire Downs, a Mob-controlled thoroughbred racetrack in western Massachusetts that was co-owned by Patriarca and Philadelphia Mob boss Angelo "The Gentle Don" Bruno.

That night at Roseland, Wigfall knocked out Perry, a Virginia fighter, in the first round. Fighting out of Vecchione's Ward 5 stable, Wigfall fought seven more times that year, including three times in May alone, and ran up a record of 8-0 with six KOs. Like Marvin, he was fighting as frequently as possible, not only to make money, but also to move up in the middleweight division, which was suddenly crowded with rising contenders.

The Brockton High gym would become a home field for Marvin as he fought five fights there in 1973 and 1974. After that first pro fight against Ryan, he had two other fights, both victories, before it was time for him to face Wigfall. Marvin was haunted by the beating he took in Crescent Court and wanted redemption.

Marvin's legend was growing fast, as was the rivalry between the Petronelli Brothers and Vecchione. The two camps competed for fighters and their boxers were regularly pitted against one another. The two camps kept score of their wins and took great pride in their victories. As Marvin became a star, Vecchione realized the mistake he made ignoring Marvin when he came into his gym.

"Hey, that's how it goes," Vecchione once said. "Whaddaya want from me? If he boxed I woulda seen what he had but all he did was sit. How did I know what he was sitting on?"

Marvin was 3-0 with two KOs in his new pro career. The stage was set for a clash that went down in history as one of the biggest grudge matches in Brockton lore. It was set for Brockton High School on October 6, 1973.

As Marvin prepared for the fight, Goody was wary of his young fighter's mindset. Goody was from the old school. He was a true student of the sport. He came of age in a time when boxing was ruled by gentleman like Jersey Joe Walcott, Joe Louis, Floyd Patterson and his friend, Rocky.

He understood and respected the urban anger that built inside young boxers like Marvin, but he did not accept brutish behavior, insubordination, laziness, cockiness, or, most of all, disrespect for the sport. He also accepted no shortcuts and led by example, working out alongside his fighters as he trained them.

Marvin was just learning the craft as he trained for his fight against Wigfall. To Marvin, it was the biggest moment of his life—a chance to redeem himself and reclaim the pride that was stolen from him in Crescent Court that night a few years earlier. Marvin trained hard and was focused, but Goody grew concerned that Marvin's commitment was being driven more by revenge than a desire to become a great boxer. He feared Marvin would be overcome with the emotion of the moment, be too eager or angry, and implode under the pressure.

"Marvin," he told his young fighter, "Boxing is not the venue to seek revenge. It's not a place for ego. Anger and a lack of discipline here in my gym, or out there in some ring in some other city, I don't give a shit where it is, is how you lose. The quickest way to end your career in this sport is to fight for the wrong reason. You fight because you love it, you respect it, and you eat, sleep, and drink it. Any other reason, and you're in trouble."

Marvin listened intently, as he was starting to do more and more with Goody and Pat. He was starting to trust them. They gave him a job, taught him to box, and helped him turn pro. They also listened to him but, most important, they did not ask him for anything other than his best.

"I'm here to become world middleweight champion. That's why I'm here," he said.

Marvin was just eighteen but he was already signing autographs for kids in the gym, calling himself "Future Middleweight Champion." It was not bravado. It was his mission.

Goody looked at him sternly and replied, "Well, if you're serious kid, so am I."

Silverman promoted the fight and packed the Brockton High gym. The buzz leading up to the fight was enormous. The gym was jammed, mostly with Wigfall fans who watched him dominate on the BHS gridiron and believed he was similarly headed for boxing stardom.

Many had heard about the street fight and thought Marvin was overmatched. Wigfall was the star in Brockton, not Marvin. There were more than a few there that night who wanted to see Wigfall put the new kid from Jersey on the canvas. Few had seen Marvin box but most had heard about him being on a mission to avenge the parking lot beatdown.

"Marvin was an outsider," says Jack Cashin, who was in the gym that night. "Everyone knew of him. It was street talk. The Brockton people there at the fight thought Wigfall would kick his ass."

"It was a packed house. It was just electric," Cashin remembered. "Most of the people were for Dornell. We were all rooting for Dornell."

But the fight did not go the way the crowd or Wigfall expected. Marvin had learned to fight. The Petronellis had taught him well. He took out one of the toughest kids the Shoe City had ever seen, disposing of him in a lopsided contest that somehow went eight rounds. It should not have lasted that long as Wigfall was brutally beaten around the ring by the younger, faster, stronger, and tougher fighter.

"It was a big shock," said Cashin. "Dornell showed glimpses of greatness. Marvin just wore him down. He got inside and he wanted it more."

Years later, Marvin recalled the fight and said the beating he suffered in Crescent Court drove him.

"I never let that die," Marvin said. "Every time I had the chance to put him out, I let him back into the fight. I whupped him, right in front of all the people who had seen him deck me that night. It might take me three years, but I'm gonna gitcha!"

The decidedly pro-Wigfall crowd cheered wildly for Marvin as he pulled off the upset.

"Marvin made a name for himself in Brockton, beating him," Cashin said.

He also won his biggest purse to date: $1,000.

BOSTON GARDEN

Dornell Wigfall looked to be on his way to a good pro career, but the beating from Marvin that night at Brockton High set him back. He lost his next fight to Willie Taylor, a light heavyweight from Brooklyn, who knocked out Wigfall in the sixth round in New Bedford. Wigfall was reeling from the Hagler defeat and losing to Taylor only drove him further down into dysfunction. He was drinking, smoking, and working more and more for the local wiseguys rather than training.

Despite losing back-to-back fights, he was booked in January 1974 to fight Italian light-heavyweight champion Emmio Cometti in Milan. Fighting for Vecchione had its perks, which included ties to mobsters who often influenced matchmakers. Milan was a long way from Crescent Court but Vecchione had faith Wigfall could turn his career around with a big win against an international champion.

Vecchione turned to his friend, legendary manager Al Braverman, to set up the fight. Braverman would soon go to work for Don King. Pitting a tough, young Boston fighter like Wigfall against an Italian champion would get some good press, especially if Wigfall could pull off the upset.

It was a huge opportunity for Wigfall to take his fight career to the next level. But his personal life was a disaster and the pressure was too much. He went MIA.

Two days before the fight, a panicked Vecchione called Braverman in New York and told him Wigfall was not going to Italy to fight. He could not find a replacement on such short notice and told Braverman to call off the fight.

"Are you kidding?" Braverman said. "This is for a fight against the Italian light-heavyweight champion, and it's been advertised all over the country. Vinnie, if somebody doesn't show up, they'll kill us both!"

Braverman told Vecchione he had better find a solution—quick. What happened next is one of the most legendary and wildest tales in boxing history. Vecchione, a trainer who had never fought a pro match, took a boxing license from one of his other fighters, a light heavyweight named Paul Poirier.

Poirier, from New Bedford, Massachusetts, lost his father in a house fire when he was nine. His mother died of a brain hemorrhage two years later. An uncle steered his orphaned nephew to boxing and Poirier started training with Vecchione at the Ward 5 gym. He sparred frequently with Marvin, as well as Wigfall, and turned pro when he was just fifteen, using a fake birth certificate to get a professional boxing license.

After seven straight wins, the Massachusetts Boxing Commission found out Poirier was underage and tried to strip him of his license. Local state Senator William "Biff" MacLean of New Bedford stepped in and passed special legislation allowing Poirier to continue pro boxing. At age seventeen, he was the youngest fighter to ever box at Boston Garden when he knocked out Jesse Bender in the second round.

After a few more fights, Poirier abruptly retired, saying he wanted to finish high school. He was planning to return to the ring when he graduated at age twenty, but he and his adopted family joined the Jehovah's Witnesses, a strict religion that barred him from prizefighting.

Fortunately for Vecchione, the retired Poirier left his license behind at the Ward 5 gym. With no other option left, Vecchione grabbed Poirier's license, hopped on a plane to Milan, and went to the weigh-in, posing as Poirier. No one noticed and Vecchione climbed into the ring against Cometti.

The Italian champion had his way with "Poirier," the Milan newspapers reported. He beat Vecchione over four rounds before the fight was stopped. Vecchione flew back to America with two black eyes—and $600 for the beating. The scam was never uncovered and Poirier never knew what Vecchione had pulled off until years later.

A few months after Vecchione's fight against Cometti, Braverman went to work for Don King. Braverman was a plug-ugly ex-heavyweight with a mashed nose who managed several fighters, including heavyweight contender Chuck Wepner. It was Braverman who set up Wepner's fight against Sonny Liston that ended with a nine-round defeat and Wepner needing a hundred stitches. The massacre underscored Wepner's nickname: "The Bayonne Bleeder." After the fight, Liston was asked by a reporter if Wepner was the toughest guy he ever faced.

"No," Liston said, "but his manager is," referring to Braverman.

After the Liston fight, Braverman matched Wepner with Muhammad Ali. It was the fight that inspired Sylvester Stallone's film, *Rocky*. Ali had just beaten George Foreman in the Rumble in the Jungle and needed a tune-up fight. Braverman and King brought him Wepner, a journeyman and massive underdog. The fight was held March 24, 1975, at Richfield Coliseum just outside of Cleveland.

The run-up to the fight was a circus as Ali hammed it up on TV, falsely claiming that Wepner called him racial epithets. Ali knew interest was low because Wepner was a 10-1 underdog, but he hoped whipping up racial tensions would get fans to tune in to see if the six-foot-five-inch lumbering white guy could give him a fight.

Wepner, who was paid just $100,000 to Ali's $1.3 million, did just that. After eight intense rounds marked by claims and counterclaims of rabbit punches to the back of the head, the fighters tangled and Ali fell to the canvas in controversial fashion.

Ali shrugged off the knockdown and ratcheted up his intensity. He pounded Wepner for the next five rounds. Wepner made it to the final round but was knocked down and the referee stopped the fight, giving Ali the TKO victory.

Wepner later gave Stallone one of the most memorable lines in the film. He told Stallone that the night before facing Ali he lay in bed with his wife and told her: "Even if I don't win, I just want to prove I belong there."

In the movie Rocky repeated it to Adrian before he faced Apollo Creed.

A year after the Ali–Wepner fight, Braverman cashed in on his fighter's underdog status and matched him against wrestler Andre the Giant in an exhibition at New York's Shea Stadium. It was another stunt that Stallone used as inspiration, pitting his character Rocky against Thunderlips, played by Hulk Hogan, in *Rocky III*. The Wepner–Andre the Giant match devolved into chaos as Braverman punched wrestler Gorilla Monsoon during a ringside brawl.

Braverman continued to work with Vecchione—and Dornell Wigfall. The two managers remained lifelong friends. Wigfall resurfaced after Vecchione filled in for him in Italy and went back into the gym. Vecchione put aside the mishap and set up a string of fights for him. A month after the Milan charade, Wigfall scored a knockout against New York light heavyweight Bob Green at Don Bosco High School in Boston.

Marvin, meanwhile, went on a tear in 1973, beating whoever was put in front of him. He fought two more times at Brockton High, knocking out Hartford fighter Cocoa Kid and Cove Green of Bridgeport, Connecticut, before traveling to Portland, Maine, on December 6, 1973, to battle Lowell light heavyweight Manny Freitas. Freitas got knocked down three times in the first round before the fight was stopped.

Just twelve days later, Marvin fought New York's "Panama" James Redford at the Hynes Convention Center in Boston. Tony Petronelli was also on the card. Goody and Pat's fighters had a cachet that ratcheted up the disdain between them and the Ward 5 camp. Silverman played on the rivalry, poking Vecchione every chance he got, while promoting the Petronelli brothers' fighters heavily before a Christmas-week event at the Hynes.

"Petronelli and Hagler are probably the two best fighters in the country from one area," Silverman told reporters before the fight. "You'll see a couple of very exciting fighters in these two kids."

Silverman's boasting did not go over well at Ward 5, but it paid off. Tony Petronelli, then the New England welterweight champion, scored a unanimous ten-round decision over "Irish" Pat Murphy of New Jersey, while Marvin knocked out Redford in the third round.

The win was a turning point for Marvin. It was becoming clear that not only was he better than the fighters at Ward 5, he also had the most potential of any fighter in Goody and Pat's stable, including Tony. Silverman took note and slotted Marvin on the undercard of a middleweight title fight at Boston Garden between Tony Licata and one of Marvin's childhood heroes, Emile Griffith. Born in St. Thomas, Virgin Islands, and raised in New York, Griffith was a five-time world champion who held the welterweight title three times and the middleweight crown twice.

Marvin once told reporters that when he pretended to box as a kid in Newark, he envisioned being Floyd Patterson or Emile Griffith. Now, he was going to fight in the same ring as one of his idols.

Griffith was a standout middleweight but was struggling. He was 77-16 going into the Licata fight and had a rocky stretch the previous few years that included two losses to undisputed middleweight champion Carlos Monzon. In June 1973, Griffith fought Monzon for the WBC, WBA, and *The Ring* magazine titles, losing a fifteen-round unanimous decision to the champion. Six months later, in Paris, Griffith lost another unanimous decision to Australian bruiser and pro rugby player Tony Mundine.

The truth is, Griffith was never the same after his controversial, and ultimately tragic, 1962 nationally-televised fight at Madison Square Garden against Cuban Benny Paret. During the weigh-in, Paret caressed Griffith's buttocks and whispered in his ear "maricon"—Latino slang for "faggot"—incensing Griffith. Griffith worked as a fashion designer at a women's hat factory at the time and later came out as bisexual.

The champion punished Paret over twelve rounds before the fight was mercifully stopped. But it was already too late. Bloodied and battered, Paret was rushed to the hospital, where he died a week later. Griffith never got over the fatal beating and later said it haunted him for forty years.

None of it mattered to Suitcase Sam, who billed Griffith–Licata as a battle for the open WBC and NABF middleweight crowns. Griffith was still a marquee name at the time, despite his spotty record, so getting Marvin on the undercard was a coup for Goody and Pat. He was matched up against Bobby Harrington, a rangy New York fighter who had a record of 16-18. But it was Marvin's biggest fight yet as the attention of the boxing world was on the Griffith bout.

Before the fight, Pat Petronelli had arranged a sparring session with Griffith, but Griffith's trainer, Gil Clancy, canceled it after watching Marvin train.

"Marvin was so disappointed," Pat Petronelli recalled. "He kept saying he just wanted to spar. He wouldn't even try to hurt him. It would just be an honor to be in the ring with Griffith. He couldn't understand."

Undeterred, Marvin sparred anyone else who dared take the gig. He stayed focused on the task at hand. He was still on the undercard for one of his heroes. He marched into the Garden before a hometown crowd and destroyed Harrington, knocking him down twice in the fifth round before the fight was stopped, which gave Marvin the TKO and his eleventh straight win. Griffith lost a twelve-round decision to Licata, who was just two years older than Marvin.

Griffith fought seventeen more times after that night at the Garden, losing eight of them, including two losses to boxers who would become pivotal to Marvin's future: Italian-born New Yorker Vito Antuofermo and Britain's Alan Minter.

Boarded-up building in Newark in August 1967 at the height of the race riots.

TIME OUT — John William Smith (left), 41, the cab driver whose arrest last July sparked the Newark riot, and his lawyers, Harris David (center) and Oliver Lofton, are shown during recess during Smith's trial for assaulting two arresting officers. The two officers stopped Smith's cab for allegedly tailgating their patrol car, and, after a scuffle, he was arrested. A rumor spread through Newark that Smith had been beaten to death and violence broke out shortly afterward.

News clipping of John Smith.

Rocky Marciano.

Marvin and Tony Petronelli at Petronelli Gym in Brockton circa 1973.
Courtesy of Tony Petronelli

Marvin's early rival, Dornell Wigfall, at Ward 5 Gym in Brockton. *Courtesy of Jay Sergio*

Newspaper advertisement for Marvin's 1974 rematch against Olympic gold medalist Sugar Ray Seales in Seattle.

Program from Marvin's 1976 fight at The Spectrum against Willie "The Worm" Monroe.
Courtesy of J Russell Peltz

Telegram from Pat Petronelli to promoter J Russell Peltz agreeing to terms for the 1976 Willie Monroe fight.
Courtesy of J Russell Pel

Program from Marvin's 1976 fight at The Spectrum against "Bad" Bennie Briscoe. *Courtesy of J Russell Peltz*

The Triangle—(left to right) Goody Petronelli, Marvin, Pat Petronelli. *Courtesy of John Merian Jr.*

(left to right) Marvin's sister Noreen aka "Buttons," Marvin, Marvin's mother Ida Mae, heavyweight champion Jersey Joe Walcott and Marvin's sister Cheryl aka "Sherry." *Courtesy of Artie Dias*

Marvin with Bob Arum (center) and John Merian Sr. *Courtesy John Merian Jr.*

Two powerful Massachusetts politicians—U.S. Senator Edward M. "Ted" Kennedy and U.S. Rep. Thomas P. "Tip" O'Neill, who was then Speaker of the House of Representatives—pressured Bob Arum to give Marvin a shot at the middleweight title.

British middleweight champion Alan Minter. *Courtesy of Elizabeth Minter*

Alan Minter receives a hero's welcome back home in Crawley, England, in 1980 after defeating Vito Antuofermo to win the middleweight title at Caesars Palace in Las Vegas. *Courtesy of Elizabeth Minter*

National Front posters such as these were plastered around London in the late 1970s.

CRAWLEY, ENGLAND

Across the Atlantic Ocean, in 1962 in Crawley, England, a small town in the west end of the county of Sussex, a young boy, just eleven, wandered into Crawley Boxing Club on Station Road with his father Sydney, a rugged plasterer and World War II veteran.

Trainer John Hillier was a flyboy in the British Royal Air Force as well as an amateur boxer. While in the service, he began training fighters and in 1958 he started the New Town Amateur Boxing Club. Much like Goody Petronelli, he focused on training young men serving their country. Goody trained Navy servicemen while Hillier was the trainer for countless British Sea Cadets stationed at the port.

After a year or so of mentoring successful amateur fighters, Hillier was recruited to run the Crawley Boxing Club, where he built a stable of tough, young fighters that included Bob Edgeworth, Clint Jones, and Johnny Pincham. Much like Goody and Pat had no idea what walked into their gym in 1969, Hillier was equally unaware of what Alan would become one day: the most successful fighter to ever walk through his doors.

Born on August 17, 1951, in the Southeast London suburb of Penge, in the Bromley borough, Alan Sydney Minter was the eldest son of Syd Minter, a plasterer, and his wife Annalisa, a German-born stay-at-home mother.

Alan was blessed with his mother's blue eyes, which made young women in Sussex swoon as he aged but struck fear in his opponents in the ring.

He spent the first two weeks of his life in an incubator.

"Yes, I was dying," Minter once said. "I had my last rites read to me and everything. They got the vicar in and they said 'He won't survive. He won't come through.'"

His parents met while Sydney was serving in the British Army during World War II. He and Anne built a life south of London, in a rural farming village, where Alan and his brother Mick, who was five years younger, spent their days running around the stables. Much like Marvin and his sister Veronica, the Minter brothers were inseparable, often left to roam the village together while his father worked and his mother took care of the home.

"It wasn't rough. We had a nice upbringing," Mick Minter says. "We played a lot on the farm. It was a family friend's farm."

Like Marvin, Alan was protective of his younger sibling and took on bullies who picked on Mick.

"He looked after me," Mick Minter says. "I had a worse temper than him. He never had a temper."

The boxing bug came to Alan from his father, who was an amateur boxer during his military days. Syd Minter was also a hard drinker, which made for some rocky times for the family.

"He was a hard man. He was a drinker from London and he was the governor wherever he went," Mick recalls. "He made sure he was in charge. He was a tough guy. If he'd had a drink, it was sometimes tough. We respected him."

Syd's plastering company did well. The family was working class and, while money was sometimes tight, they were not wanting for much. Syd and the men who worked for him loved football, darts, and a nice pint. After a long day of work, they retreated to the local pub, often for long hours.

While Alan and Marvin would not know each other's names for a decade, there were similarities between them. Like Marvin, Alan quit school young. He dropped out at age fourteen, once telling reporters, "I think I must have had the school record for getting caned."

He fought so much in school that the headmaster directed him to the boxing ring, which he had first been introduced to by his father.

"I was always in trouble," he said. "I spent most of my time being put outside the classroom."

It was well known in school that Alan was boxing. He would come into school on a Tuesday, fight that night, and skip class the next day because he had bruises and cuts on his face. There was one teacher, his gym instructor, Mr. Hansom, who Alan credited with him staying in school as long as he did. While the kids teased him for being marked up from fights, Mr. Hansom was supportive.

"One day, I'm in school on a Wednesday, in assembly, and [Mr. Hansom] . . . said, 'He must have won his first fight. Alan Minter, stand up,'" Minter recalled. "So I stood up and the whole school applauded and cheered. It had never happened to me before, but it happened then, and that was it. That's what made me carry on. I've always said it's sad for children who are doing something and they don't get a pat on the back."

With Mr. Hansom and his father cheering him on in the gym, Alan's mother too was supportive, although she worried about her son as his boxing career began.

"I remember when I went home after boxing with black eyes, all banged up, and my mother cried her eyes out," he remembered. "But she never once said to me 'You don't want to do that.' She never said nothing."

Young Alan followed in his father's footsteps working as a plasterer, while training for the ring. It was not unlike Marvin's journey of quitting school and going to work as a laborer for the Petronellis, although Alan was lucky enough to have a father around to help him navigate his future.

Alan started fighting amateur and got off to a rough start, losing his first three bouts. But he stuck with it. Like Marvin, he too was a southpaw. He was tall, fast, and had power, but he was a bleeder. Fighting out of the Crawley club, he won twenty-five of thirty amateur bouts. He was named southern England's area champion four times. While his official amateur record shows just nineteen bouts, he fought a reported 145 amateur fights, winning 125.

It was in May 1970 when Alan earned his ring name "Boom Boom." He was representing England at the Multi-Nations tournament in Holland, and fought a young man named Peter Lloyd, from Wales.

"I used to make this grunting noise when I threw a punch and the referee kept warning me, 'Don't make that noise. You're making the noise again. If you keep making that noise, I'll disqualify you,'" Minter recalled. "But it was a habit and, even if I didn't throw a punch, the noise was still coming out."

His powerful punches, coupled with the grunts, prompted people in the crowd to start chanting "Boom Boom!" It stuck and remained his moniker for the rest of his career.

"I would climb into the ring, all the crowd would shout 'Boom Boom!' and it was lovely," Minter recalled.

Mick finished school and their father opened a drinking club in Brighton, while Alan rose quickly through the British middleweight ranks and was named to Great Britain's 1972 Olympic team. Alan was building cupboards on a job near the family's Crawley home when his father tracked him down to tell him the news.

"It was funny, because I've got to the Olympics and I'm still working for my father's plastering company, still in the cupboards," he recalled. "So my dad's come round to the site to tell me that I've had a letter to say I've been picked for the Olympics and he couldn't find me because he didn't know which fuckin' cupboard I was in! When he did manage to find me, the whole site closed down. Everyone got booze in and we had a party because I had just been picked to represent my country."

What awaited him in Munich was not only a shot at Olympic glory, but a piece of history that shocked the world.

MUNICH

In August 1972, Alan packed up his gear bag, with his red-and-white Great Britain Olympic shorts and tank top, and made the trip to Munich for the Games.

Going into Munich, Alan was seen as the class of the light-middleweight division and was considered Britain's best hope for gold. The local papers named him one of the entire British team's favorites to medal, not to mention restore the UK's boxing reputation globally.

But the boxing gods had other plans.

Upon arriving in Munich, one of the first people he encountered in the Village was a young man named Sugar Ray Seales—a fighter he and Marvin would soon get to know very well. Born in the US Virgin Islands, Seales grew up in Tacoma, Washington, and was a menace in the amateur middleweight ranks in the early '70s, which landed him a spot on Team USA's star-studded team in Munich. Seales breezed through the light-welterweight division, winning five bouts by decision, none of which were close, and won gold for Team USA. He was a fighter on the rise and turned pro immediately following the Games. Seales would soon become a middleweight and later fight Alan and Marvin.

Alan's Olympic experience was different. His brother, Mick, and his father, Syd, made the thirteen-hour road trip from Crawley to Munich in the family Volkswagen. They bunked down in quarters in the Olympic Village as part of Alan's entourage. Syd was proud of his son's transformation from plasterer to world-class athlete and working-class hero in the pubs of Sussex. Alan, just twenty-one, took the praise in stride.

He made his Olympic debut on August 30, 1972, at Olympiahalle in Munich against Guyanan Reggie Ford. He beat Ford easily, knocking him out in the second round. The Birmingham, England, newspapers hailed the Sussex fighter after the victory.

"He almost lifted Guyanan Reginald Ford off his feet with a right hook," the *Birmingham Post* wrote of the fight. "Ford could only shake his head and blink . . . It was one of the best punches thrown in the lively Olympic tournament."

Next, Alan fought Russian Valery Tregubov, a brawler who came into the second-round fight riding a wave of controversy. Two days before he faced Alan, Tregubov was beaten up badly in a match against Marine Cpl. Reginald Jones, from Marvin's hometown of Newark. Jones was a tough boxer thought to have a bright future in the sport.

A year before the Olympics, in just his second amateur bout, Jones won a unanimous decision over Leon Spinks, who would go on to win gold as a light heavyweight in the 1976 Olympics in Montreal and defeat Muhammad Ali in 1978 to become undisputed heavyweight champion.

But the judges in Munich did not seem to think much of Jones. Despite the undeniable beating Jones gave, the judges awarded a 3-2 decision to the Russian. The bout was televised live on ABC with commentary from Howard Cosell, who castigated the verdict.

The decision set off a near-riot in the Olympic arena as fans threw cans, food, and trash into the ring, an unusually crass and embarrassing display for an Olympic event. The raucous crowd booed for fifteen minutes and became increasingly unruly. Alan saw the decision and knew Jones was robbed.

Emboldened by the victory, Tregubov fought Alan at the Olympiahalle on September 2, 1972. Tregubov was a two-time European amateur champion and was nine years older than Alan.

"He's a bit of an old warhorse now," Alan told the press before the fight. "I think I can handle him."

Handle him he did, winning a unanimous three-round decision over the Russian that turned out to be the last fight of Tregubov's career. He left Munich and returned to Russia where he died two years later at age twenty-eight.

Two nights after beating Tregubov, and with a day off, Alan, his brother Mick, their father, and Alan's trainer, Doug Bidwell, along with some teammates, hit the pubs of Munich to celebrate Alan's twenty-first birthday.

Security in the Village was lax. The German government reduced fencing and softened the military presence, making it easier for athletes to come and go. They even had unarmed Olympic security officers wear approachable, light blue uniforms, in stark contrast to the gun-toting brownshirts under the Nazi regime. It was a calculated attempt by the German Olympic Committee to create a more relaxed environment as it sought to erase images from Adolf Hitler's 1936 Olympics, during which Nazi propaganda was plastered everywhere and the country was a cold, dystopian police state.

Mick Minter said security was so soft that he used an ID with a photo of British boxer Maurice Hope, who is Black, as he seamlessly came and went unchecked from the Village.

The relaxed approach turned out to be a catastrophic mistake. While Alan and his crew drank lager in the pubs of Munich on September 4, eight machine gun-wielding Palestinians in a terror group called Black September slipped into the Village and stormed the Israeli team's flat. The mask-wearing guerillas killed a wrestler and a coach who tried to fight them off and took nine hostages. The terrorists demanded that Israel release two hundred Palestinian prisoners, but Israeli officials refused, citing their policy not to negotiate with terrorists.

Gunfire rang through the Munich night as the German Olympic Committee quickly realized it had made a devastating miscalculation. The Israeli team had raised concerns during the Games about a lack of armed security but their fears were ignored. When the gunshots erupted, those unheeded fears became a tragic reality.

As Alan and his soused-up entourage returned to the Village, they were surprised to see that it was locked down. Helicopters whirred overhead. Armed soldiers stood guard and barred Alan and his teammates from reentering the Village to go to bed in the British dormitory.

"We went out to Munich and I had my twenty-first birthday out there," Alan told a biographer years later. "All the trainers and everything, we all went out for the night and it was brilliant. When we got back to the Olympic Village, we couldn't get back in. All the doors and gates were locked. The security was phenomenal. There was helicopters, guys with machine guns, and we couldn't get near. There had been a terrorist attack."

What was unfolding inside would become one of the darkest chapters in Olympic history. The tense standoff between the German police and military and the Black September commandos lasted nearly two days. A group of reporters, including Howard Cosell, *Washington Post* reporter Shirley Povich, and *Los Angeles Times* sports columnist Jim Murray, snuck through barricades and reported from inside the Village throughout the crisis.

In a 1987 *LA Times* column, Murray described the surreal scene inside the Olympic Village.

"Rock music blared from a hundred cassettes, ice cream stands did a lively business, pin-swapping was endemic, gymnasts practiced back flips, runners jangled, couples danced. It was hard to believe that a few hundred feet away in Building 31 on Connollystrasse, a handful of other young athletes sat bound and blindfolded on the floor, under the guns of eight terrorists. On the floor lay two colleagues, one dead, one dying."

As the crisis intensified, unbeknownst to the Olympic revelers, West German police snipers opened fire on the hostage-takers. The gunmen responded by executing the Israelis, putting bullets in the heads of eight of them and killing the ninth by tossing a grenade into an escape helicopter. When the violence subsided, there were six Israeli athletes and five Israeli coaches dead, along with a West German police officer and five of the eight terrorists.

Cosell and co-host Jim McKay stayed on the air live throughout the tense hostage situation. There were erroneous early reports that the hostages had been safely released before McKay grimly broke the news to the world at 3:30 a.m. that the Israelis had been killed.

"They're all gone," he said somberly.

The Munich Massacre shook the world as it was the first hostage-drama in history to play out on live TV. The violence changed the Games forever and prompted many countries to form counterterrorism agencies. Alan and his entourage were shocked by the news and unsure when or if the competition would resume. Alan had a date with Algerian Loucif Hamani, but had no idea if he would be fighting again in Munich.

He got his answer within hours. Shockingly, the tragedy delayed the Games only temporarily. Just a few hours after McKay's report, International Olympic Committee President Avery Brundage told the world at a press conference that "The Games must go on." A memorial was held for the Israeli victims the morning of September 6 while athletes from around the world—including Alan—reported to their respective venues and got back to competing for medals.

The Israelis, however, did not. The whole team was flown home under orders from the Israeli government as their nation mourned and the Israeli elite special-reconnaissance unit—known as the Sayeret Matkal—plotted retribution.

The three members of Black September who survived the gun battle were arrested and sent to a West German penitentiary. In another stunning turn of events, the trio were released to Palestinian authorities just a month later in a hostage exchange during the hijacking of West Germany-bound Lufthansa Flight 615. Their Black September comrades hijacked the Boeing 727 when it left Syria bound for Munich and threatened to blow up the aircraft unless the three terrorists were released and the terror group was paid a $9 million ransom. Israel again refused to negotiate but West German authorities complied. The three terrorists were set free while the hijacked Lufthansa plane was flown to Tripoli where the crew and all twenty passengers were released unharmed. The terrorists were greeted as heroes upon their return to Libya and paraded before the media as freedom fighters.

The exchange infuriated Israel and sparked its twenty-year "Wrath of God" covert operation that targeted thirty Black September members and associates for assassination, including many top leaders of the Palestinian Liberation Organization. It is believed, but never confirmed, that two of the Munich terrorists were tracked down and killed by Israeli commandos, while the third was last known to be hiding in Northern Africa.

In 2022, the German government acknowledged failing to protect the Israeli athletes in Munich and awarded the victims' families a $28 million settlement.

Alan, like all the athletes, was shaken by the violence and it haunted him for years. He put aside the chaos, however, and headed back to the Olympiahalle for his next bout. The British sailing team won gold that morning, which gave Team UK a morale boost. Alan was a bit groggy from drinking, but he shook off the hangover and laced up to fight Hamani. In the second round, Alan was warned about his habit of grunting heavily with every big shot he threw. The crowd booed and responded by mimicking Alan's grunting in unison throughout the rest of the fight. By the end, the crowd was on his side, chanting "Boom Boom!"

Energized by the fan support, Alan outclassed Hamani to earn a 4-1 decision. Hamani turned pro a year later and went on to have thirty pro fights over ten years. Among them was a 1980 second-round knockout loss to Marvin in Maine.

With the victory, Alan advanced to the medal round and was matched with Germany's Dieter Kottysch, who was eight years older than him. Wearing his white-and-red Team UK shorts and tank top and white gloves, Alan fell behind in the first two rounds as the German fighter landed punches that did little damage but scored points for the judges.

In the third round, Alan's blue-collar grit and punching power took over. He knew he was behind and came out swinging, hitting Kottysch with shots that snapped his head back. The heavily German crowd, sensing the onslaught, started chanting "Dieter! Dieter!" but it only ignited Alan. He fired combinations at Kottysch's head and caught him with a big right hook that knocked him to the canvas. It got worse for the German as Alan smelled blood. He continued his assault, hitting Kottysch with shot after shot.

"Kottysch is in real trouble as Minter goes for him," the British announcer said in the final seconds of the fight. "All Minter at the finish."

As the final seconds elapsed, Alan hit him with hard overhand lefts and brutal right hooks that nearly knocked Kottysch down again. Kottysch barely survived the round and it appeared Alan would be headed for the gold-medal match. But that didn't happen. Instead, the judges delivered a stunning decision that favored the German by a score of 3-2.

As the scorecards were read over the public address system, Kottysch kept his hooded head down, seemingly resigned to defeat, until the decision was announced that declared him the winner. He screamed in joy and leaped in the air, appearing surprised that he had won. Alan bowed his head in disgust and disbelief. It was a disgraceful decision not unlike the robbery Reggie Jones experienced two days earlier.

"He never won that fight, and the crowd knew he was beaten," Alan later recalled. "I'm standing there and they announced the majority decision to him. He jumped up in the air, and I just couldn't believe it. The crowd booed and jeered and, when they presented me with the bronze medal, the crowd erupted again because they knew."

Kottysch went on to win gold while Alan went home to England, bitter and angry that he had been robbed. He had been anointed Britain's boxing savior and felt like he let down his countrymen. It would not be the last time he would carry that massive weight and feel that disappointment.

He had taken the responsibility of being a national representative seriously and trained as hard as he had in his life. To have victory stolen from him with such blatant injustice was not easy to accept. The press agreed he had been robbed. It was a difficult ending to Alan's amateur career, but his performance also put the middleweight division on notice.

Alan turned pro shortly after returning to England. He made his professional debut at the Royal Albert Hall in London on Halloween 1972, defeating Maurice Thomas in the sixth round by TKO. It was the start of a collision course with Marvin—and history.

FRIDAY NIGHT FIGHTS

While Minter tore through the ranks in Europe, Suitcase Sam ramped up his efforts for Marvin, Goody, and Pat. As Marvin rose in the middleweight division, a buzz grew about the young kid from Brockton and his two middle-aged Italian managers. None of them were household names.

Marvin had not fought in the Olympics. He was not part of Bob Arum's or Don King's stable. He was not selling out arenas in Las Vegas and he was not fighting on ABC. He was the antithesis of a media star. He was also a devastating puncher with an excellent chin who scared off a lot of fighters.

Goody and Pat, meanwhile, were running their construction business by day and the gym in Brockton by night, fostering Tony Petronelli's career, and working with some other local prospects. While nationally Marvin was not getting much attention, locally he was becoming a draw as the Boston sports media took note of the dangerous middleweight knocking out guys from Portland to Providence.

In 1974, Silverman partnered up with Boston sports radio host Eddie Andelman, a bespectacled and rotund everyman with a brutal Boston accent who bled New England Patriots red, white, and blue. A Dorchester-born graduate of Boston University, Andelman was also a rabid horse racing fan who socialized with trainers and promoters and may have liked to lay a wager or two.

He was a pioneer of local sports talk radio who in 1969 founded *The Sports Huddle*, a weekly talkback show on WEEI-AM radio that focused on the Patriots, Celtics, Red Sox, and Bruins, during a time when Boston sports mostly left the region depressed rather than planning championship parades. Andelman was the face of the trailblazing show, which created the blueprint for modern talk radio in Boston and nationally.

A sharp-tongued, wisecracking, and often painfully-blunt analyst, Andelman parlayed the success of the radio show into a local TV gig on WNAC-TV Channel 7. The CBS-affiliate, located at Bulfinch Place in downtown Boston next to Faneuil Hall, was one of just three networks on TV in Boston at the time, along with ABC and NBC.

With his gap-toothed smile and sardonic wit, Andelman was a popular media personality who started on the city's NBC affiliate WBZ, before he moved to WNAC. In addition to his TV and radio gigs, he was a philanthropist who raised lots of money for Boston charities, including the Jimmy Fund. He organized the popular "Hot Dog Safari" at Suffolk Downs racetrack, which attracted a who's who of Boston athletes, politicians, business leaders, and celebrities.

He was also a huge boxing fan and a savvy promoter. He knew there was a ton of local boxing talent from Lowell, Brockton, the North End of Boston, and South Boston that would bring eyeballs—and advertising dollars—to WNAC. So he launched a live TV fight series and included Marvin in some of his first cards. The fights were held in a ring set up in the station's Bulfinch Place studio.

The WNAC fight series sought to capitalize on the growing interest in live boxing on TV, inspired by the huge television audiences of ABC's *Wide World of Sports*, which aired fights on Saturdays, as well as the 1973 rematch between Muhammad Ali and Ken Norton, which was broadcast on ABC.

On April 5, 1974, Suitcase Sam and Andelman set up a Friday Night Fights card at WNAC that pitted Marvin against Tracy Morrison, a light heavyweight from Kansas City. Tony Petronelli fought on the undercard in a welterweight rematch against Lowell fighter Beau Jaynes, who Tony had lost to just three months earlier. Tony won a unanimous decision over Jaynes, setting up a possible sweep for the Petronellis.

Admission was fifty dollars per ticket, a portion of which went to charity, which was an expensive night at the fights in 1974. The ticket prices, coupled with the TV studio's proximity to Boston's toney Beacon Hill neighborhood, helped draw an upscale, black-tie crowd.

A *Boston Globe* boxing writer described the scene, saying: "Not many women there knew a right cross from an uppercut and a few winced and covered their eyes as Hagler drew blood and finally stalked his man into submission."

Morrison lasted eight rounds before a bad cut opened up on his eye, prompting the referee to stop the fight, giving Marvin his twelfth straight win. It was also his first win on live TV.

"It was a good fight for me," Marvin said after the victory. Of fighting under the bright lights of TV, he said: "You have to concentrate on the ring. Take your eyes off of your opponent to look at the crowd, and you're in trouble."

Marvin fought four more times over the next four months, including twice in May, winning all by KO. It was around this time that Marvin and Bertha made a decision that would forever change Marvin's image: they decided she would shave his head before big fights.

While he was known around Brockton for his tight Afro and his nickname, "Stuff," his cleanly-shaven head would become his trademark for the rest of his career. He shaved his head every two weeks using a Gillette Trac II razor, while Bertha did the honors before fights.

She also started learning about boxing, immersing herself in the sport, and hanging around the Petronelli Gym more where she would serve as timekeeper, sounding the bell at the end of every three-minute round. She would sometimes bring the children to the gym and talk to Marvin about what she saw him doing right and wrong.

"I tell him, 'Make sure your hands are up,' or 'You dropped your left hand,'" she said.

They had a deep connection and trust in those early days in the mid to late '70s.

"We did a lot of things together. We talked about a lot of things about his fighting career," she says.

One of the middleweights standing in Marvin's way was another rising star, Olympian Sugar Ray Seales. Seales had fought seven times in 1974, winning them all—five by KO. Suitcase Sam, Goody, and Pat knew Marvin was ready for a big fight and wanted to match him up with Seales.

Sam went back to Eddie Andelman and they set a main event back at the WNAC studio. Marvin was 14-0 while Seales was 21-0. Seales was the top welterweight in the world at the time and moved up to fight Marvin because no one in his normal weight class would fight him. He was viewed as a heavy favorite to beat Marvin, despite Marvin's undefeated record and growing knockout power.

Seales was running his own gym in Tacoma and taking drama and public speaking classes at a local community college in between fights. Goody and Pat knew how good Seales was and were certain he would come into the Boston fight in top condition. It was common knowledge that Seales viewed the fight against Marvin as a tune-up to get to higher contenders and bigger purses.

"I'll go wherever I have to, fight whomever I have to to become the champion," Seales said before the fight.

The bout was a charity fundraiser for the United Way, which drew another capacity crowd at the TV station. Silverman upped the interest in the fight by announcing before the match that the winner would face unbeaten Tony Licata for a $10,000 purse.

The fight was a major step forward for Marvin as he was taking on not only an Olympic gold medalist, but another undefeated fighter who was as hungry as he was for a world championship. A year earlier, while still fighting amateur, Marvin lost in the National Golden Gloves semifinal to Seales's brother, Dale Grant, in Lowell, Massachusetts. But at 21-0 as a pro, Marvin was a very different fighter than he was in Lowell.

He was obsessed with perfecting the techniques Goody taught him. Goody studied the fighters Marvin would be facing and emulated them in the ring while he worked the mitts with Marvin. He mimicked their styles, punches, and tendencies, educating Marvin on how to counter and exploit their vulnerabilities. Goody was masterful at preparing Marvin, while also keeping him grounded and focused.

When he walked toward the ring at WNAC that night he was ready. Flanked by Goody and Pat, he wore purple velour trunks emblazoned with white letters "MMH"—Marvelous Marvin Hagler. He entered the ring to cheers from the 250-plus fans, bouncing confidently but solemnly, his eyes focused across the ring at Seales as he dripped sweat.

Seales, by contrast, was shivering cold. It was August in Boston, but Seales and his team wondered if the promoters had cranked up the air conditioning in his locker room to freeze him out before the fight.

"We never knew anything about Marvin Hagler, not me or my team. But we sat in the studio [in Boston] waiting to go out to the ring, and I was freezing, cold solid," Seales recalled years later. "Hagler came out and he was dripping in sweat. I feel we were bamboozled. My promotional team at the time, they didn't know what they were doing."

The cold apparently did not affect Seales much, however, as he came out strong in the first round. He punched with precision, stinging Marvin with a few sharp jabs and winning the round on points.

Marvin settled in and went to work in the second round and caught Seales with a hard right that nearly sent the Olympian to the canvas. Seales recovered but the fight turned into a slugfest that Marvin controlled the rest of the way. Seales's nose bled from the second round until the final bell, while his right eye swelled up and nearly closed from Marvin's punishing blows. Marvin won a unanimous ten-round decision, the biggest victory of his career up to that point. It was also the first time he ever went the distance in a fight.

"He'll go far," Seales predicted after the fight. "He surprised me."

Marvin said he was "nervous" beforehand but locked in after Seales started trash-talking in the beginning of the fight.

"He tried to out-talk me at the start, like Clay [Muhammad Ali]," Marvin said. "I'm not a talker. I just felt like I was a better fighter."

Seales made $1,500 for the fight while Marvin made $1,000. One sportswriter praised the fighters for putting on a show and said future bouts at the TV studio needed to pay the combatants more.

"The fighters will have to get more money, if last night's good battle is any indication," the *Boston Globe* wrote.

Globe sportswriter Leigh Montville covered the fight at WNAC, describing it as "like going to *American Bandstand*."

"It was a strange thing," Montville recalled.

Seales, Montville believes, underestimated Marvin and paid a price.

"Sugar Ray didn't know what he was getting himself into," Montville said. "He came in and Marvin pounded him. Sugar Ray was surprised by the whole thing. He thought he was going to go in and just be a celebrity."

Seales was taken by cab to nearby Mass General following the beating, where he received stitches.

After the convincing win made national news, few would underestimate Marvin again.

HAGLER–SEALES II

The televised fight drew huge ratings for WNAC and got widespread media coverage. It proved to WNAC and promoter Eddie Andelman that there was demand for live boxing on TV, so he planned more fights. He invited actual boxing fans to the Hagler–Seales fight, as well as scantily-clad ring girls, which was a departure from the upscale crowd at the black-tie charity bout Marvin fought in his first time at the TV station. The result was a more authentic, more engaged fight crowd that resonated with fans, viewers, and the press.

"A big mistake we made the first time was that we didn't have a boxing crowd. It was too reserved, too quiet," Andelman said. "This time.... We had the boxing people here. We've got the hot dogs, the free beer, the chips. We're trying to make everyone loosen up, to forget they're on television."

Televised fights were just taking off at the time and Marvin was one of a handful of young fighters poised to take advantage of the emerging media platform, with his bravado, bald head—which one writer compared to *Kojak* star Telly Savalas—and inspiring life story of escaping Newark. Pat Petronelli for one saw the potential before them.

"I just hope this leads to some real money," Pat said.

Added Andelman: "Television can revive boxing now. These kids were seen by three-quarters of a million people tonight. Can you beat that exposure?"

Following the fight, stagehands immediately started to clean up the mess in the studio because it needed to be spotless for the next live broadcast from the station: Sunday's Catholic Mass.

Like Andelman, Silverman saw the potential in the success of the broadcast. *Friday Night Fights* on TV and closed-circuit broadcasts in the '50s and '60s were popular.

"It's a stepping stone," Silverman said. "Boxing needs help and I'm glad that a TV station is trying to help."

The broadcast gave much-needed publicity to Marvin, as he sought a shot at Licata or another top contender.

"He's strong and he can fight," Silverman said of Marvin. "And we wouldn't have found out if we hadn't had the show on TV. This Seales never would have come here if he hadn't been on the tube. So it was a good move."

Following the Seales win, Marvin fought two tune-up fights at Brockton High over the next few weeks while Seales fought once, knocking out Les Riggins in the second round in Seattle, before a rematch was announced.

Silverman was a pioneer in securing lucrative broadcast deals for his fights, and Marvin, thanks to the win over Seales, was starting to become a draw, even though he, Goody, and Pat were outsiders in the notoriously insular and crooked fight game. Silverman and his partner, Rip Valenti, were hustlers. They knew Marvin had star potential and would attract real money as long as he kept winning. The middleweight division was an afterthought in the sport at the time, as the boxing world was focused mostly on the heavyweight division, which was packed with stars, including Muhammad Ali, Joe Frazier, George Foreman, and Ken Norton, among others.

The lower weight divisions simply did not draw the interest of the general public like the heavyweight division did. What the middleweight division needed was an American star—an intimidating assassin with knockout power. Someone like Marvin.

Silverman and Valenti were not sure Marvin was that fighter, but they were certain he could beat most, if not all, of his contemporaries. And they could fill some arenas along the way.

The rematch with Seales was set for November 26, 1974, just three months after their first fight. But this time it was on Seales's turf at the Seattle Center Arena. Silverman and Valenti promoted the fight and negotiated a TV deal to have it broadcast back to Boston from Seattle.

Interest in the fight increased as the promoters announced a rubber match would be held should Seales win, possibly at Boston Garden. Marvin had no intention of having that fight as he was determined to keep his undefeated record.

The Friday before the fight, Marvin and Seales appeared together at a press luncheon where each predicted victory.

"I'm going to win and it's not going to last ten rounds," Seales boasted.

"I'm gonna knock him out this time," Marvin retorted. "I was a little too careless the first time. This time I'm not messing around."

The fight was another battle. Seales was the aggressor in the early rounds, stinging Marvin with jabs to his face. But Marvin proved too strong and too tough, taking over from the sixth round on, lacing Seales with lefts and rights that again bloodied his nose and swelled up his right eye. Seales clutched Marvin in the late rounds and danced away from his punches, hoping to steal a late round or two. In the tenth, Marvin rocked Seales with a hard left that nearly knocked him down. Seales would later say the punch made him "see stars."

But when the judges' scorecards came in, the fight was declared a draw. Seales needed butterfly stitches to close a cut beneath his right eye while his lips and face were badly swollen. Despite looking like he'd been in a head-on collision, Seales argued that he won the fight on points.

"I thought I won the decision," he told reporters while icing up his face in the locker room. "Sure, I'm sort of disappointed, but I improved over the last time I met him. Hagler is a good fighter."

Marvin chalked it up to a hometown decision. He was furious and thought he had beaten Seales beyond any doubt.

"I know I won it," he said. "But I'm three thousand miles away from home and I know that if I'm gonna win I have to do it up good."

After the fight, Silverman said Marvin was robbed and that "even the hometown Seattle papers reported" that he won. Silverman was not too mad, however, because he held the contract for a lucrative third fight between the two.

It was the first controversial decision Marvin had experienced as a pro fighter. But it certainly would not be his last.

CUTS SLOW DOWN MINTER

Back in England, Alan Minter was struggling. He lost his final two fights of 1973, both due to gashes over his eyes that could not be closed, requiring the fights to be stopped.

Cuts were becoming a major problem for him and would haunt him the rest of his career.

In 1974, things did not get any better. He fought six times that year, winning three and losing three. Two losses came at the hands of Jan Magdziarz, a Polish national who lived in Southampton, England. A few weeks before Marvin and Seales clashed in Seattle, Alan fought Magdziarz a third time but both were disqualified in the fourth round for "not giving their best."

The fight was an embarrassment to the sport. Alan was fearful of being cut again, so he kept his distance the entire match. Magdziarz seemed equally content to not engage, so he danced and clutched. Barely any punches were thrown. The few that were lobbed were light flails that barely grazed the other fighter. The referee gave them three warnings before calling the fight in the middle of the fourth.

The crowd at Royal Albert Hall in Kensington jeered and booed. Dozens walked out in disgust. The TV announcer called the fight "a disgrace." The winner was supposed to get a shot at the British middleweight title but neither did because of the debacle.

Alan later admitted that he was embarrassed by the charade.

"We were both disqualified, both slung out of the ring," he said. "I'll tell you what, he had that right hand and it was so fast and straight that he couldn't miss me with it. I shouldn't have fought him. Every fighter has a bogeyman, and he was mine. He was coming forward and I went back. I was coming forward and he went back, and neither of us threw a punch. The crowd was going berserk."

A month later, and just a few days after Seales and Marvin fought to a draw in Seattle, Alan returned to Munich for the first time since his Olympic disaster. But this time it was different—he scored a unanimous decision over Luxembourg's Shako Mamba. It was a big win for Alan to end the year and gave him momentum going into 1975 as he had four wins in the first few months of the year, two by knockout.

Meanwhile, back in the States, Sam Silverman took Marvin, Tony Petronelli, and Dornell Wigfall to Boston Garden in December 1974 in what proved to be a tune-up for Marvin for a rematch against Wigfall. The Christmas-week card at the Garden featured Petronelli in the main event and both Marvin and Wigfall on the undercard.

Wigfall fought in the first fight of the night, hammering a fighter named Kenny Jones so badly that he refused to come out for the third round. It was a big win for Wigfall, who seemed to be resurrecting his career despite his vagaries. Vecchione had him focused—or at least more focused—and he was always well conditioned. Wigfall was 6-1 since losing the decision to Marvin at Brockton High in October of 1973.

Marvin, meanwhile, moved past the Seales heist and scored a second-round TKO over Bridgeport, Connecticut's D.C. Walker. In the main event, Tony Petronelli knocked out Johnny Copeland, an Irish brawler from St. Louis, in the sixth round to and improve to 26-1. It was a stellar night for Silverman and the Petronelli brothers and for Vecchione and Wigfall, who was promised a rematch against Marvin.

Wigfall fought at Boston Garden again a month later, earning a unanimous decision over Tracy Morrison, the San Francisco fighter Marvin beat a year earlier in the WNAC studio in Boston. The victory cemented a grudge rematch between Marvin and Wigfall on February 15, 1975.

The fight would be back at Brockton High. Marvin and Goody lived in the gym for weeks before the fight. They had heard about Wigfall's personal problems but he was on a winning streak and still formidable. There could be no letdown.

Marvin bought into Goody's strict training regimen. Goody was a nutrition freak who believed there were no shortcuts to being in top physical condition. Goody ran alongside Marvin as he did ten miles of roadwork daily. In the ring, Goody kept pace with Marvin working the pads for endless rounds until both were drenched and exhausted.

"You could tell he was a fighter. He was always in there dancing with Marvin. Good footwork," Steve Joyce—whose father, Mike Joyce, was one of Marvin's cornermen—remembers of Goody.

Mike Joyce was a secret weapon of sorts for Goody and Pat. Mike would scout fighters across New England, looking for any with championship potential. He also was expert at identifying fighters' tendencies and vulnerabilities. Over the years, he gave Goody invaluable insight in training camp as well as at ringside.

"I'd sit and watch those two work a corner in a fight. Goody and my father would go back and forth about what they were doing right and wrong. They would know real quick," Stephen Joyce recalled.

Mike Joyce was that guy every gym and every successful fighter needs. He was knowledgeable about the fight game and did whatever needed to be done out of a love for the sport. He carried spit buckets for Marvin early in his career and was Goody's sounding board, confidant, and friend. He had keys to the Petronelli Brothers Gym and often took the lead training other young fighters so Goody and Pat could focus on Marvin.

"I don't think my dad ever got paid a red cent," Stephen Joyce says. "My father was never doing it for the money. He loved boxing, the gym, all of it—just being around it. When you love something that much, you don't do it for the money."

Marvin, too, loved Mike Joyce. Just as he trusted Goody and Pat, he also trusted Joyce, not only for his boxing expertise but also as a mentor. When Marvin threw huge family cookouts at Romuva Park in Brockton, the Joyce family was there with the Petronellis, Marvin, Bertha, and the kids. Bertha became close friends with Mike Joyce's wife, Patricia. The two young mothers helped each other out watching each other's kids while Marvin, Mike, and the Petronellis were off at the gym or traveling for fights.

Stephen Joyce said Goody often pulled him aside as a kid at the gym and gave him valuable nutrition and health advice.

"He'd say, 'This is what you gotta do. You gotta take care of your nutrition. It's all about diet,'" he said. "You've gotta eat your fruits and your protein."

Goody would be sweating as hard as Marvin at the end of workouts. As a former fighter himself, he knew the importance of stamina, strength, flexibility, and endurance. Goody was no young man—he was fifty-two in 1975—but clearly prioritized his own physical fitness. While Pat gambled, played the ponies at the racetrack, and liked to drink, Goody was a teetotaler who rarely, if ever, drank alcohol, got eight hours of sleep, and ate three healthy meals a day. And whether working out with Marvin or on his own, his regimen never changed.

"Goody tried to keep himself in as good a shape as he could. He wasn't a young guy," Stephen Joyce said.

His methods were also ahead of their time. While Tom Brady has made flexibility, "pliability," and reducing inflammation the cornerstones of his bestselling *The TB12 Method*, Goody was using similar techniques, although simpler, back in the mid-'70s with Marvin. He worked on Marvin's flexibility constantly. He stretched Marvin out endlessly. Marvin would do a thousand sit-ups in a session. And at the end of each four-hour training session, Goody would give him a full-body massage with Bengay.

"The whole room would smell like Bengay," Stephen Joyce recalled. "I would ask him why. He'd say 'To keep his muscles loose.' Goody would talk about getting rid of inflammation. Goody was smart. He knew his health and was ahead of his time."

Dornell Wigfall, however, was not maintaining such a rigid and disciplined lifestyle. He was naturally strong and a gifted athlete, but he drank heavily, smoked cigarettes, and was more interested in Cadillacs, women, and the gangsterism surrounding the Ward 5 gym and Brockton's East Side. Three nights before the rematch with Marvin, Wigfall went missing. He had not shown up for training for two days, so Vecchione went looking for him, eventually tracking him down in a motel in nearby Halifax, Massachusetts, drunk and surrounded by empty bottles.

Vecchione cleaned him up, put him in his car, and drove him back to Brockton. Vecchione got his fighter a room at the Bryant Hotel in downtown Brockton and stayed with him the night before the bout to make sure he stayed clean and was ready to fight.

Despite his erratic behavior and lax training, Wigfall was again the favorite. Most of the crowd was once again rooting for him. He showed up to the Brockton High gymnasium shortly before the fight in sunglasses and a flashy, camel-hair trench coat and stood up in front of the stands.

"I'm here!" he bellowed to wild cheers, throwing his hands in the air.

Wigfall cut Marvin's eye early in the fight. Had Wigfall been in better condition, he may have capitalized and closed out Marvin that night. A few more shots to that eye, and the fight may have been stopped.

Instead, Marvin's strength, speed, agility, punching power, and ring IQ were too much for Wigfall. Marvin stalked Wigfall, ignored the cut, and took control of the fight. He was no longer the scared kid cowering under the car at Crescent Court.

Besides toughing it out, Marvin also had a secret weapon: Goody was one of the best cutmen in the business. He was a former Navy medic who knew how to stop bleeding like few others. No one knew for sure what Goody used to close Marvin's cuts, but it's likely it would not be legal today, and probably was not back then.

Regardless, it worked that night. Marvin survived the cut, knocked Wigfall down in the sixth, and won by KO. The gym erupted into mayhem as Wigfall was counted out. Family members and friends from both sides hopped into the ring and started brawling.

"It was one of those things," Wigfall's brother, Charles, recalled of the post-fight chaos. "Everyone there was on one side or the other."

Wigfall and Marvin escaped the dustup and fled to their respective locker rooms, while Brockton cops broke up the melee. The fighters showered and left the gymnasium, once the coast was clear. Both camps ended up at a Brockton nightclub later that night where they made peace and celebrated.

"My brother congratulated him and bought him a bottle of champagne," Charles Wigfall remembers.

It was a memorable night but after that post-fight party at the club, Marvin had little interaction with Wigfall ever again. Marvin's career took off, while Wigfall's spiraled downward.

Wigfall was gentlemanly in defeat, but the beating he took that night at Brockton High marked the beginning of the end for him. He fought three more times in 1975 and 1976—winning them all by KO. But his career was derailed when he was arrested for an armed robbery in Rockland, Massachusetts, in 1976 and sentenced to three years in prison. He was released in 1980, claimed he was a born-again Christian, and returned briefly to the ring.

He had four pro fights in 1981, winning three, including one at Boston Garden. The one he lost was a TKO to a nobody named Tony Campbell from Buffalo at Wonderland Ballroom, an ornate and smoky arena inside a mobbed-up dog track in Revere, Massachusetts. Wigfall fought three more times, losing two.

His final fight was on Friday, March 18, 1983. at the Convention Center in Atlantic City, on the undercard of a Michael Spinks fight. Spinks was 22-0 at the time and won a fifteen-round decision over Dwight Muhammad Qawi to become the unified light heavyweight world champion. Wigfall faced South American Cruiserweight Champion Jose Maria Flores Burlon. He fought hard but was knocked down in the third and lost by TKO in the eighth. It was the last time he would ever fight in the ring.

He returned to the streets of Brockton, unfortunately, and eventually wound up back in prison—for most of the rest of his life. On February 9, 1988, he and two other men visited the home of twenty-six-year-old Luis Colon, a Boston man who had just moved to Highland Street in Brockton a few months earlier. Sometime around 6:30 p.m. that night, Colon was shot multiple times after three men entered his home. Colon survived but was paralyzed by the gunshots and confined to a wheelchair.

Wigfall always claimed he was not the shooter who paralyzed Colon. During his 1989 trial in Brockton, two witnesses backed his claim. Still, a Plymouth County Superior Court jury convicted the once-promising prizefighter of armed assault with intent to murder, armed robbery, and weapons violations. He was sentenced to twenty-to-thirty years in state prison.

Leaving the Brockton courtroom after the trial, Wigfall told reporters he was framed.

"They know I was innocent," he said. "They've been doing it to me all my life, even through my fight career, and this time it was checkmate."

Dornell Wigfall's losses to Marvin haunted him in prison. He later claimed he beat Marvin in their first fight but was robbed by the judges. He also said the second fight was stopped prematurely after he was knocked down. He said the referee saved Marvin, who was bleeding from a cut.

"The second fight was really all-out taken from me," Wigfall said. "How can you take a fighter—when his opponent's hurt—stop it and give it to the man who's bleeding?"

"The referee counted ten when I was on my feet," he continued. "He was hurt and they stopped the fight and gave it to him."

Despite being hit with a long state-prison sentence, Wigfall had ideas of opening a gym in Brockton upon his release. He claimed to be working out young fighters in Plymouth House of Correction and was looking forward to getting them fights.

"When I watch them, it makes me smile," he said.

Wigfall's cell at MCI-Concord was plastered with news clippings from Marvin's fights. He claimed he was framed and obsessed over what could have been. Marvin's success drove him mad.

"He had a real chip on his shoulder. He just thought he was better," friend Jack Cashin says. "But he was in jail and Marvin was on the way to the top. He lived that dream, thinking he would get out and fight Marvin again. But that never happened."

Wigfall claimed in later years that his football and boxing career were unfairly derailed by his arrest before his senior year at Brockton High for assaulting a police officer. He claimed he was innocent of that charge, which led to him being kicked off the football team. Brockton lore is that he took the rap for one of his brothers, but never fingered anyone.

"That's when my career started turning around, when they took me out of football," he said. "I was going to college . . . They didn't give me no break."

In 1999, while serving a twenty-year sentence for shooting Colon, he sued the State of Massachusetts and the Department of Corrections after officers sprayed him with chemical agents during a shakedown. In court filings, Wigfall repeated the claim that he was wrongfully convicted. His family has also insisted he was wrongfully convicted.

Wigfall lost his suit against the DOC and served out his sentence. He was released from jail around 2011, and fell back into old habits, hanging around Gigi's Lounge. He died on February 5, 2014, at Signature Brockton Hospital at age fifty-nine. He had four children and in his obituary his profession was listed as a "self-employed landscaper."

After their second fight, Marvin was focused on goals far beyond Brockton, telling the *Boston Globe*: "I don't think anyone will go around saying I'm not the best in New England."

He mentioned several other contenders he wanted to fight and added: "They had better fight me now, because the longer they wait, the more dangerous I become."

Goody, too, used the victory to taunt top contenders. He knew that he, his brother, and Marvin would have a tough time getting big fights, mainly because they were not part of the machine run by promoters Don King and Bob Arum.

Goody used the media after the Wigfall fight to push the boxing press to take note of Marvin in hopes of forcing the sports' power brokers to match him with true contenders.

"He's right to fight anybody . . . they've been ducking us," Goody said.

MINTER ON THE MOVE

A few months after Marvin Hagler disposed of Dornell Wigfall once and for all, Alan Minter faced one of his toughest opponents, Kevin Finnegan, a warrior who would give Alan three hard battles and also give Marvin all he could handle.

In May 1974, Finnegan was himself a surging contender in the suddenly-crowded middleweight division. He won the European middleweight title in Paris via a unanimous, fifteen-round decision over France's Jean Claude Bouttier. A few months later, he beat Mexican Eddie Mazon at Royal Albert Hall in Kensington, before putting his Euro title on the line against West Germany's Frank Reiche. The fight was a war and revealed Finnegan's toughness. It went ten rounds and Finnegan won a decision, despite suffering a broken jaw that required surgery. Just six months after his surgery, he traveled to Italy, where he lost his title in a fifteen-round decision to Italy's Gratien Tonna, another middleweight contender.

At the same time Alan was on a five-fight win streak after the embarrassing double disqualification with Magdziarz, which set up the match with Finnegan. It was a homegrown battle that captivated the British boxing world as the two UK middleweights, both of whom were contenders for the world title, took the risk and fought each other. Both were on course to fight Marvin and enter the top ten, but they also wanted respect from the British press and the boxing world. Both were at different times considered Britain's best hope to restore respectability to British boxing and win the world middleweight title.

They first squared off at Empire Pool at Wembley Arena on November 4, 1975. Going into the fight Finnegan was 24-3 while Alan was 19-4. The fight was for the vacant British middleweight title. There had not been a bigger fight in Britain in many years. The pubs emptied into Wembley to see which local hero would emerge victorious.

Finnegan was a hard man. One of eight children of a laborer and an Irish mother, he grew up in Buckinghamshire and trained under legendary British trainer Freddie Hill at Craven Arms Gym in Lavender Hill in South London. His brother Chris won Olympic gold in 1968 in Mexico City. The brothers were legendary drinkers who regularly popped into the pub below their gym for several pints of Guinness. Chris also fought pro and once was suspended from the sport for eighteen months after he jumped into the ring to contest a decision against his brother.

Minter–Finnegan lived up to the hype as it went fifteen grueling rounds. Alan won a unanimous decision and was lauded by the British press.

"It was a performance far above his usual standards," the UK's *Evening Telegraph* said in the next day's paper. "Minter . . . boxed beautifully."

A year later, they would have a rematch at Royal Albert Hall in Kensington in a second battle for the British middleweight title. Alan won another 15-round decision. Finnegan, undeterred, fought four more times over the next year and won all four bouts.

As tough as he was in the ring, Finnegan was an equally talented artist. He was a painter in the style of classic French Impressionists. His work was good enough that he had showings in London's prestigious Mayfair gallery district. After his boxing career, he divorced his wife, Marilyn, and ran a bar in Spain.

He later lived in France and sold his art to cafes, hotels, and bars. He was open about his battles with the bottle, once saying: "I boozed my way through £250,000 in five years . . . I had a great time but unfortunately I don't remember half of it."

He was sometimes homeless in his later years. He was missing for several days in 2008 before he was found dead in his London flat. He was sixty.

Following the Finnegan fights, Alan had a tough stretch. He fought contender Tony Licata at Wembley just two months after the second battle with Finnegan. Licata lost to world middleweight champion Carlos Monzon a year earlier by TKO in the tenth.

Alan met Licata on November 9, 1976, at Wembley Arena and won by TKO in the sixth. Less than a month later, Alan was matched with fellow '72 Olympian Sugar Ray Seales at Royal Albert Hall. Finnegan fought on the undercard and won, putting himself in position for a third shot against Alan, should Alan beat Seales.

It was not an easy affair. Alan was struggling with cuts during his fights. He had lost several bouts due to bleeding, including many in which he was up on points. He was a good fighter but that did not matter if he kept getting cut. If a glove busted open his face and blood flowed, the bout was getting stopped and Alan would get the loss.

Alan had lost too many fights that he should have won because of lacerations and he was sick of it. He was keenly aware that his fight career would soon be over if he could not avoid cuts. So he went to see specialists, including a hypnotist and a boxing consultant, in search of answers.

"He looked at me, and could find nothing wrong with my face or the bones. He said the reason you're getting cut is because you're getting hit," Alan recalled. "That advice cost me five hundred quid! But I suppose I was fighting like a lunatic. It became a bit of a phobia. You train for months and months and the fight's stopped on a cut. It's heartbreaking."

With no answers from the professionals, Alan put aside the laceration issue and prepared for his fight with Sugar Ray Seales. A few days before the fight, he met the British press and talked about Seales's bravado.

"As soon as we met he started to psych me," Alan said. "We were having our photograph taken and all the time he kept telling me how he would knock me out."

"I had to tell him to grow up," Alan concluded.

Seales's cockiness drove Alan that night at Albert Hall. He was behind after the first three rounds, had a cut above his eye, and an egg forming on his forehead. Alan knew he had little time before the referee would stop the fight, so he stepped it up in the fourth and fifth rounds and brought the fight to the American.

He dropped a beaten-up Seales to the canvas in the fifth and the fight was stopped, giving Alan the win.

"That was the first time I've ever been knocked down, let alone stopped," Seales said.

Alan knew he had fought well, but was surprised Seales went down.

"The left hand I got him with was so fast I didn't even realize I'd tagged him with it," he said.

Following the fight, Alan had to go to the hospital to have his swollen forehead lanced and drained. The doctors examined him closely and reviewed his medical records, which by that time were filled with notes about sutures, cuts, recurring facial wounds, and scarring. Alan was cleared, but the issues would follow him for the rest of his career.

For Seales, the defeat was another difficult loss that dropped him in the rankings. Nevertheless, he kept fighting. Just like Marvin and Alan, Seales believed he was the class of the division and coveted a world title. It put him on a collision course with Marvin. But it would be two years before Seales and Marvin met a third time. It was not worth it to either of them, or their managers, to have a third bout until one or both of them was at the top of the division.

The focus of the sporting world at the time remained on the heavyweights but true boxing fans knew that many of the world's best boxers were middleweights. Marvin, Goody, and Pat were aware the division was highly competitive so they strategized carefully about when and where to fight to capitalize on the attention the division was getting.

While the British and Europeans battled across the Atlantic, Marvin, Goody, and Pat scrambled to find a way to separate themselves and get Marvin a world title.

Up to that point, Marvin's biggest purse was $2,000. No one wanted to fight him because he was a southpaw and because he had a reputation as a killer in the ring.

"Look, I can't get Hagler no fights," Silverman told Pat.

Pat, ever the gambler and totally confident in Marvin, told Silverman to make any fight he could. Marvin would fight anyone.

"Try and get him licked if you want," Pat said.

"You mean that?" Silverman said. "I got a guy who's gonna lick him."

That guy was "Mad Dog" Johnny Baldwin, an undefeated southpaw from Houston. The fight was held at the Hynes Convention Center in Boston. Tony Petronelli, who was once the star of the Petronelli gym, now appeared on the undercard of Marvin's fights.

"He used to carry my gear up the stairs at the gym," Tony said. "But pretty soon, I was carrying his bag for him."

Tony was 30-1-1 at the time and won by tenth-round TKO. Also on the undercard was Dicky Eklund, a Lowell fighter and brother of Micky Ward. The brothers' story was later made famous in the Academy Award-nominated film *The Fighter*, with Mark Wahlberg playing Ward and Christian Bale showstoppingly playing Eklund. Eklund was just starting his pro career and was 3-1 and won a unanimous decision. He compiled a 19-10 pro record before drug addiction ended his career.

At the Hynes, Marvin dominated Baldwin to win a ten-round unanimous decision. Still, he sought the respect he believed he had earned. Marvin's management needed to make a move.

So, with the guidance of Suitcase Sam Silverman, the Brockton boys headed south to Philadelphia.

PHILLY

"Philly?" What the fuck are we going to Philly for?" Goody asked his brother Pat.

Pat was a gambler's gambler. He loved to play the ponies at Suffolk Downs, the pups at Wonderland and Raynham Park, and would occasionally take a trip to Saratoga, Aqueduct, Belmont, or anywhere else that had bettting windows and scotch. Pat also loved hitting the tables in Atlantic City and Vegas whenever they were there for fights. He loved the action and loved striking deals. Besides a blackjack table, a bargaining table was one of Pat's favorite places to be.

"If we want Marvin to fight the best, we have to beat these fuckin' guys," Pat said.

"Pat, Philly is tough for a Boston kid. Never mind a Brockton kid," Goody said.

"Sam says otherwise," Pat said. "It's time."

Goody was skeptical, not only because he knew wars awaited Marvin there, but also because he thought there were more fights to make in Boston, Providence, and Europe. But Sam and Pat convinced him to go..

"If we were going to get anywhere we had to fight 'The Iron.' So we went to Philadelphia," Goody later recalled. "All those Philadelphia fighters were tough. I called them 'The Iron' because they were as tough as iron."

Waiting down in the "City of Brotherly Love" for Marvin was a murderer's row of hungry up-and-comers tired of beating on each other looking for weaker opposition. To them, and their promoters, that was Marvin.

J Russell Peltz, a sportswriter-turned-boxing promoter, controlled Philadelphia boxing in that era. He was the matchmaker that Goody and Pat had to deal with to get Marvin into the Spectrum and out of the New England minor leagues. Portland, Boston Garden, and Providence were good for a paycheck, but at the Spectrum Marvin would make or break his career. It was a gamble, but Pat wanted it and Marvin and Goody trusted his instincts.

"When he came into Philly in January '76, we were the center of middleweight boxing in the world," Peltz said.

Marvin's first trip into the lion's den went poorly. He was 25-0 when he, Goody, and Pat drove south to Philadelphia to face Bobby "Boogaloo" Watts, a South-Carolina-bred fighter who was the first cousin of Jimmy Young, a heavyweight contender who beat George Foreman and also fought Muhammad Ali and Ken Norton.

Watts was a country boy, born in a barn in South Carolina and a descendant of slaves. His parents, Clarence and Corrine Watts, were sharecroppers. They had six kids. Bobby was their fourth. He worked the farm as a young boy, picking cotton and stacking peanuts and corn. When he was ten, his parents decided to leave their sharecropping life behind and moved the young family to Philadelphia.

It was a tough transition for young Bobby.

"Life in the country was hard work but I liked it," he wrote in a self-published memoir in 2007. "I got homesick because I missed running around in the woods, doing the barn work, and walking around with no shoes on my feet."

A year after arriving in Philadelphia, things got even harder when Bobby's father died. His father was a drinker and one night passed out on a stoop, hit his head, and died of a massive brain injury. It only made life harder for Bobby and his family as they tried to assimilate to the hardscrabble streets of South Philadelphia.

In junior high, he got bullied often and mugged a few times. Sometimes neighborhood gang members would sucker punch him and steal what little money he had on him. He grew tired of it so one day he followed his cousin Jimmy to the Police Athletic League gym where he started to box.

"You had to be able to hold your own," Bobby wrote. "I wanted to be able to walk the streets and take care of myself. So by me going to the gym, I started to get a lot of respect."

It was a tough upbringing but it prepared him for the battles ahead with Marvin and other top middleweights of the era. Bobby turned pro in 1969 and was 27-3 when he met Marvin at the Spectrum. Marvin was 25-0-1, the draw being with Seales. But the Philadelphia fighters were not scared of him. Philadelphia was the locus of boxing talent at the time and New England was not viewed as a place that produced great fighters. Marvin changed that perception, but it would take time.

Marvin was cocky in his early days. He worshiped Ali and sometimes danced and preened in the ring to taunt his opponents. He was not, however, a natural showman.

"When I first started, I used to dance around like Muhammad Ali," Marvin recalled in his later years. "Every fighter starts out cocky. Then they find out what confidence is."

Marvin was still that cocky young fighter on January 13, 1976, when he met Watts at the Spectrum. He also had helped raise Bertha's two kids and now she was six months pregnant with their first child, a son they would name Marvin Jr.

Both Bertha and Marvin came from large families. Just as Marvin had helped raise his younger siblings, Bertha also assumed a parental role at a young age while growing up in Randolph, Massachusetts, and later Brockton.

"It's not too hard. I raised most of my sisters and brothers," she told a reporter in 1981.

With no father around, Marvin often became a de facto parent to his younger siblings. Now that he had a newborn and two young kids at home, it was normal for him. He never complained and rarely showed the signs of the stress of being a young father. Goody and Pat—the only two people in the world he fully trusted—did not know the full picture of Marvin's family life or the challenges he faced.

Marvin had a family to support and was trying to create a persona to help him cash in on his ring talents. He was smart. He saw that the boxers getting press were flashy. He was not like them, but was fashioning his own image with his bald head, goatee, and me-against-the-world mentality.

He hoped the Philadelphia trip would make the sacrifices worthwhile—skipping the Olympics, working as a laborer, training nonstop. Philadelphia would make him.

He was clearly battle-tested by that point, but the Philadelphia fighters were killers. Goody knew he had Marvin ready but also knew his opponents were his equal. But he believed Marvin's killer instinct was a differentiator.

"Outside the ring, Marvin's one guy, inside he's another," Goody said. "He's a monster; the monster comes out of him. He just wants to tear his opponent apart. His words: destruction and destroy. He's not just talking newspaper talk."

Determining when that killer instinct should be unleashed was Goody's job for the next ten years. It was not known if it would be unleashed in

Philadelphia. The Spectrum was a house of horrors for most out-of-town fighters. But Sam and the Petronellis agreed this rite of passage was necessary for Marvin.

When Marvin, Goody, and Pat arrived at the Spectrum, Peltz met them.

"Guys from Boston can't fight," Peltz said to Goody, confidently.

"This one can," Goody shot back.

Peltz recalled meeting Marvin for the first time and being unimpressed.

"He came in and he spouted poetry," Peltz said.

In the prefight press conference, Marvin said he was "a cross between Joe Frazier and Muhammad Ali."

Standing before a bank of reporters, "Marvelous Marv," as the Philadelphia papers called him, delivered some playful sonnets that fell short of Ali as he evoked the memory of Rocky Marciano and his success in Philadelphia. Rocky won the heavyweight crown there in 1952, knocking out Jersey Joe Walcott.

"The Philadelphia fighters have ducked me long," Marvin started. "Now Bobby Watts will dance to my song. But he won't do the Boogaloo, only the bump in front of my shoe."

"The Spectrum crowd is in for a treat, 'cause one of their best is doomed for defeat," Marvin continued. "In the city where Rocky took the crown, another Brocktonian will go to town."

Marvin also showed a developing bitter side, reminding the media of the controversial decision against Seales in Seattle a year and a half earlier. He'd encountered boxing politics and did not like it. He was also learning that he had to use the media to his advantage whenever possible.

"They called it a draw out there, so you know I had to beat him half to death," Marvin said of the Seales draw. "When it was over, Seales came over and held my hand up to acknowledge I'd won. Then his hometown officials did a number on me."

"At least I can come away with one lesson learned," he continued. "When you fight a guy in his own hometown, don't leave him standing."

Little did he know, he was about to go through it all again. And again a few more times throughout his career. That sting from the Seattle robbery was only the beginning.

When the bell rang at the Spectrum, the six thousand fans roared for Watts, muting the Boston contingent that followed Marvin to Philadelphia. By round three, the tide was turning. Marvin hammered Watts over the first three rounds, opening a cut over his eye that started spurting blood. As Watts bled, and Marvin won round after round, the crowd began cheering in his favor.

"When the fans see blood, right away they figure the cut man is losing the fight," fight judge Earl Vann said.

Marvin appeared to have won every round. Watts stayed on his feet and landed a few punches in the last two rounds, but it seemed clear that Marvin had beaten him convincingly. He should have heeded his own poetic warning. Leaving Watts standing in his own hometown cost Marvin dearly.

When the judges' scorecards came in, Marvin lost a majority decision: two judges gave Watts the win by two rounds while the third scored it a draw. It was a disgrace that once again showed Marvin the cruelty of the boxing game.

Even the famously hostile Philadelphia crowd rejected the decision. The fans booed loudly when the scorecards were read and Watts had his arm raised in victory. Marvin received a standing ovation as he left the ring, dejected but not defeated. Goody was sickened by the scorecards.

"This town will never be the same as a fight town again," Goody fumed. "We're totally disgusted by this."

"I can't believe it," Marvin said. "I felt like I won every round. Goody told me to make sure I took the ninth and tenth rounds just to be sure, and I know I took them."

Even Peltz admitted it was a heist.

"There's no question it was a bad decision," he said. "The president of the Spectrum came down and talked to me and said, 'How could they do that?' It was either six to four or seven to three for Hagler."

The next day, the *Philadelphia Inquirer* ran the headline: "Welcome to Philadelphia Marvin Hagler."

Peltz was embarrassed and apologized to Suitcase Sam.

"I went up to him and said, 'Sam, I'm sorry,'" Peltz said.

"I'm used to it. Coming from Boston," Sam replied.

HEARTBREAK AND REDEMPTION

Marvin was down but unbowed. Bertha was home with the kids preparing for the birth of their son. Marvin never faltered, however. If anything, the robbery in Philadelphia motivated him further.

He returned to the gym where he and Goody ramped up their workouts. Student and teacher were determined to fine-tune Marvin's rapidly developing punching power and speed to make sure that next time no judges decided his fate. They were going back to Philadelphia to take what was stolen from them.

But first, in February 1976, Marvin had a quick tune-up fight at Boston Arena against a journeyman named Matt Donovan, who Marvin stopped in the second round. Just a month later—an unheard-of time frame today—Marvin, Goody, and Pat headed back to Philadelphia, this time for a ten-round fight with another of Philadelphia's best, Willie "The Worm" Monroe.

Monroe was born into a poor family in Alabama, the thirteenth of seventeen children of John and Plessie Monroe. He grew up in Crestview, Florida, and graduated from Crestview High School, before he moved to upstate New York and started boxing as an amateur at the urging of his father. He built a 43-0 amateur record and was recruited to fight out of Joe Frazier's Gym on North Broad Street in Philadelphia.

Monroe was given his nickname by iconic Philadelphia comedian/entertainer Joey Bishop, who was a member of the Rat Pack, along with Frank Sinatra, Sammy Davis Jr., and Dean Martin. The story goes that Bishop, a big boxing fan, was in Frazier's gym one day and saw Monroe fighting and said: "Who's that? He wiggles like a worm."

Monroe's trainer, Philadelphia boxing legend Yank Durham, heard Bishop and agreed, calling his fighter "The Worm" from then on. Like Goody and Pat, Durham was a World War II veteran. Durham's own amateur fight career ended when a military jeep ran him over during an air raid in England during the war.

He suffered two broken legs and was hospitalized for two years before returning to Philadelphia and training fighters that included Joe Frazier and Monroe. He spent his nights at the gym and worked by day as a union welder on the Penn Central Railroad.

It was Durham who first discovered Frazier at a Police Athletic League gym in Philadelphia and taught him to box. Under Durham's tutelage, Frazier won gold at the 1964 Olympic Games in Tokyo and became a heavyweight champion in 1968 and unified the title in 1970. With Monroe, the trainer had another potential champion who, it turns out, had the greatest performance of his life on March 9, 1976, against Marvin.

There was a blizzard in Philadelphia that night. The snow piled up so much that only thirty-five hundred fans made it to the Spectrum. Media and TV trucks could not make it to the arena, so there is no video footage of the bout.

But the press that did make it that night—as well as eyewitness accounts and Marvin's own recollections—were unanimous. Marvin got the worst beating of his career.

Boxing writer and analyst Frank Lotierzo, then a teenager, was at the fight at the Spectrum with his father. The father and son attended lots of fights in Philadelphia but almost missed the fight because of the snowstorm.

"I had no idea how we were going to get there," said Lotierzo, who lived in nearby Haddonfield, New Jersey. "My dad had a tow truck and it had four-wheel drive. So we took that to be on the safe side."

While many of his friends watched baseball games with their fathers, one of Lotierzo's earliest memories is watching the first Muhamad Ali–Sonny Liston fight with his father when he was just five.

"We never went to ball games," he says. "We went to fights."

The Spectrum was smoky and dark and boisterous. The bright lights gave it a haunting, ethereal vibe.

"You could feel it was electric and there was a sense of excitement there," he said. "The Spectrum had that aura no matter who was fighting. There was an eerie feeling the way the lights were over the ring. The ring was real white. The anticipation. It was a fight-club atmosphere, only a little bit more big time."

When Marvin and Monroe met that night, the lights bathed the two fighters as the crowd and local press got a second look at the kid from Boston via Newark who was supposedly there to beat Philadelphia's best.

"Monroe tattooed him a little bit. Peppered him around. He showed at least on that night that he was equal physically," Lotierzo says.

In the fifth round, Marvin's battered nose started pouring blood, which never stopped until the final bell. Both of his eyes were nearly swollen shut as Monroe teed off on him, slipping Marvin's jabs and throwing counters. Goody's deftness with cuts was useless as Marvin's face was busted up through to the tenth round.

"There was no question who won the fight," says Lotierzo.

When the scorecards were announced, Monroe had won a unanimous decision. It was a painful defeat for Marvin and a big setback.

"Marvin thought he was good, but he hadn't fought the caliber of fighters I had," Monroe later recalled. "He had never fought a seasoned pro. He beat Watts, but he didn't get the decision. He should have been unbeaten when he fought me."

"I was strong, tall, slick, and quick," The Worm added. "He couldn't figure me out. I hit him with a left jab in the first and his eyes opened wide. I beat him with uppercuts, busted a blood vessel in his nose. He bled a lot. Both his eyes were closed. I couldn't see how he made it through ten rounds."

While one-sided, the punishment Marvin endured impressed many observers. He could take a punch, which left many to wonder, *What would it take to knock him out?*

"He could have [quit]," Monroe's trainer, George Benton, said. "He had opportunities all through the fight and no one would blame him. But he's one tough kid. He is going to be outstanding."

"I wanted to knock him out," Monroe added. "But I couldn't."

The day after the fight *The Philadelphia News* was unforgiving.

"Philadelphia . . . has not been much of a host to Marvin Hagler this winter," boxing writer Tom Cushman opined. "Two trips here. Two muggings. Robbery in January, aggravated assault in March."

After the beating, Marvin couldn't believe that Watts had defeated Monroe.

"Can someone please explain to me how Boogaloo Watts managed to beat Willie Monroe?" Marvin asked reporters.

He was also humbled by the defeat. His confidence was tested but intact.

"I can see a great future ahead of me but I still have a few things to learn," he said. "He hit me with every punch he has. But if he'd made a mistake, he'd have found himself on the canvas."

It seemed misplaced bravado after a loss, but Goody and Pat were proud of their fighter. He took on one of the division's best, took everything he had, and walked away. They knew that despite the defeat, Marvin had taken a huge step forward.

Marvin also had business to tend to at home. A month after the fight, his son Marvin Hagler Jr. was born. The pressures of being a new father are heavy on any young man, and they certainly were on Marvin. He was working as a laborer during the day and fighting at night, struggling to break through and make a living in the ring. Bertha was overwhelmed taking care of their growing family while Marvin now had the responsibility of not only providing for Bertha and his two adopted children, but now for a newborn as well.

"I need to fight," he told Pat and Goody. "Get me some real fights. And let's go back to Philly. I can whip those cats."

Two months after "Champ" was born, Marvin returned with a fight at Roseland Ballroom in Taunton, Massachusetts, making quick work of Mississippi journeyman Bob Smith with a fifth-round TKO. He then had a rematch with D. C. Walker in Providence, which he won by TKO in the sixth.

Suitcase Sam called Peltz.

"We want Cyclone Hart," he said into the phone, referring to another difficult Philadelphia middleweight, Eugene "Cyclone" Hart.

"I know you got screwed with Boogaloo Watts, but you got your ass kicked by Willie Monroe," Peltz told him. "Three strikes and you're out."

Marvin headed back down to Philadelphia in September 1976. The city was still recovering from its Bicentennial celebration, one of the biggest parties the city had ever seen. The papers joked about Marvin being like the liberty bell—bald and with cracks. Marvin was not laughing.

He walked into Joe Frazier's Gym one day and saw Hart working the heavy bag.

"Hey, Hagler," Hart said, "I got the baddest left hook in town. Watch this."

He smashed the bag and said: "You're lookin' at the next middleweight champion of the world."

That was enough for Marvin. He felt disrespected. It was bad enough he had to abide the disgraceful decision to Boogaloo Watts, and the beating by Monroe. But now he was being taunted in a temple of boxing—Joe Frazier's Gym.

Hart was born and raised in Philadelphia. He had polio as a kid but beat the disease. He started playing basketball and running to build his legs to combat the polio symptoms. He soon found boxing, learning the craft at a local Police Athletic League gym. Boxing not only helped his legs get stronger, but also gave him tools to defend himself against neighborhood thugs.

After racking up a 29-3 amateur record, a referee gave him his nickname—"Cyclone"—because of his wicked left hook. He sparred with world champion Emile Griffith and was considered one of Philadelphia's top contenders.

Hart was a Spectrum stalwart and fought thirty-seven of his forty pro fights in Philadelphia. To say he was a hometown hero is an understatement. He was terrifying in his prime and started his career as a teenager with nineteen straight knockouts. Marvin would later say that Cyclone Hart was the hardest puncher he ever faced.

Hart was five-eleven and one of the toughest men in the division. A year earlier, he won the biggest fight of his career, a ten-round decision over Sugar Ray Seales. He also fought a war with fellow Philadelphia fighter Bennie Briscoe, earning a draw at the Spectrum in 1975. Cyclone had promise and was trained by Cus D'Amato but never became a champion. Marvin played a role in that.

A few months before the fight against Marvin, Cyclone had a rematch with Briscoe that went poorly. Briscoe hit him with a punch that broke

Cyclone's jaw and ended the fight in just one minute and forty-nine seconds.

"He has a glass jaw," *Scranton Times Tribune* boxing writer Bob Davis wrote.

Cyclone's manager, Jim Jacobs, sought to quell the glass-jaw criticism before the fight against Marvin, reminding the press that Rocky Marciano hit the canvas against Archie Moore and Joe Louis was knocked down in eleven fights.

"There's nothing wrong with Hart," Jacobs insisted.

When they met at the Spectrum on September 14, 1976, Marvin had a four-month-old baby at home and was struggling to pay his bills with his boxing purses and part-time work at the Petronellis' construction company. The pressure was intense. He could not worry about the loss to Monroe or the Watts decision. He also knew Peltz would not hand out second and third chances. He knew about Peltz's comments to Goody that said this was his last shot in Philadelphia.

A third loss in Philadelphia would be catastrophic. But Marvin wanted revenge and was ready to prove that he was the best middleweight in the Northeast, if not the world. Hart had to pay that night.

Marvin fought hard and was determined to avoid going to the judges's corecards. Before thirty-five hundred fans, most of them Hart supporters, Marvin countered, ducked, dodged, and slugged. Hart came out of his corner swinging wildly at Marvin through the first three rounds, affirming his nickname.

But Marvin was too fast and too good. He boxed with precision as Hart rushed in, knocking him down in the third round

"I tried to take him out early," Hart later recalled.

In round nine, Marvin was up on all the judges' scorecards. Hart's legs were tired. He was not well conditioned like Marvin and that took its toll.

"He had no zip," Hart's trainer, Sam Solomon, said.

When the bell rang to start the ninth, Hart did not come out. He and his trainers argued. Cyclone had enough. He signaled to referee Tommy Reed that he was a beaten man. It was over. Marvin was declared the winner.

"I just went out and I whupped him," Marvin told the press in his dressing room.

"There's no reason for a man to stay out there and take the kind of beating he was taking," Solomon said.

Before that night, the Spectrum had been Marvin's kryptonite. But now it was his place of rebirth. His career was back on course and surging as he had convincingly beaten one of Philadelphia's best.

For Hart, however, like many fighters Marvin vanquished, the loss marked the start of his decline.

"They cheered for me when I was a winner," Hart said after the fight. "Now I'm a loser and people don't like losers."

Hart would fight just twice more, losing both, including a 1977 knockout by Vito Antuofermo.

BECOMING MARVELOUS

The Cyclone Hart fight not only released Marvin's Philadelphia demons, it also led to one of the most historic runs in boxing history.

"Marvin liked to make things harder for himself," author and boxing journalist and author Tris Dixon says. "I just love the fact that he cut his teeth in Philadelphia and experienced so much there. He got such an incredible education mixing it up with those guys."

"Marvin making his bones in Philly was the making of him," he added. "It was a great place for him to go to the university of boxing."

With Goody training him, Pat handling the money, and Suitcase Sam and Rip Valenti hunting down fights, Marvin became an animal in the gym. Bertha was home with the kids while he trained at Petronelli Brothers Gym incessantly, ran up to ten miles a day, hit the weights, and conditioned his body to make sure he never lost because he was not prepared.

His training regimen was only part of why Marvin would soon become arguably the greatest middleweight of all-time.

"When you talk about Hagler, you start with the intangibles," says author and boxing analyst Carlos Acevedo. "He had ridiculous stamina, ridiculous endurance, and an iron chin. He was only officially knocked down once. And durability. You can't measure durability. He was never stopped on cuts."

When experts analyze Marvin, they often point first to him being a southpaw. But many also talk about him being a switch-hitter in the ring. He could fight orthodox or southpaw and would sometimes switch back and forth in the middle of a fight—or even a round—keeping his opponents guessing.

"He could hurt you from either side," Acevedo says. "He also had tremendous boxing skills. The first thing you notice about Hagler is his punches were compact. Pinpoint combinations. He just tore people up. He didn't have the fastest hands. But he accentuated his combinations by placing them perfectly. He was a very economical stylist."

His rough upbringing undoubtedly left emotional scars but it also put a chip on his shoulder that served him throughout his career.

"It was his lack of silk pajamas," Tris Dixon theorizes. "It was the hunger and the desire that he had for such a long time. All the adversity he boxed through, fought through, and trained through. He was a guy who embraced every type of adversity and used it as some sort of superpower."

"He seemed to thrive at having the deck stacked against him," Dixon added.

Boston Globe sportswriter Leigh Montville, who covered Marvin for years, agreed and said that there were simply no other boxers in his league at the time.

"He was a force. There were a bunch of good fighters around Boston, but none of them could take a punch like Marvin," Montville said. "He could knock people out, but you couldn't knock him down. He had a granite chin. These other fighters, they would wind up getting knocked out."

Tony Petronelli sparred with Marvin regularly in his early days. When Marvin first showed up at the Petronelli Brothers' gym, Marvin was the new guy and Tony was already well on his way to being a pro.

With Goody by their side, Tony and Marvin would often do roadwork together, running five miles in Brockton's D.W. Field Park, where Marvin ran for years. When they would spar, Marvin would sometimes pour it on so strong that Tony would have to take a break.

"I sparred with him when he wasn't Marvelous Marvin Hagler. He was just a rough, tough kid off the streets," Tony Petronelli said. "But as he got better. . . . I'd say, 'Hey, take it easy man.'"

Tony's boxing bona fides included a fight against Wilfred Benitez. What separated Marvin from the rest, he says: "Overall he was great. He was conditioned. He could box. He could punch. He could take a punch. Marvin's chin was like iron."

Legendary sportscaster and boxing analyst Al Bernstein says Marvin "had a high ring IQ" and calls him "the best middleweight I have seen in my lifetime." Bernstein saw Carlos Monzon fight, as well as later greats like James Toney, Roy Jones Jr., and Bernard Hopkins.

"I believe Marvin, in his prime, would have beaten them all," Bernstein says. "The thing that made Marvin special and maybe the thing that separated him from virtually everyone else was his dedication to the sport. No one worked harder preparing for a fight than he did. He never cut corners and his work ethic is legendary. He simply wanted to excel and refused to fail."

He was not tall—he stood just five-feet-nine-inches—but he was always the best conditioned fighter in the ring and adapted well to any type of fight. If you wanted to brawl, he could do that and made you pay. If you ran, he stalked you. If you applied pressure, he slipped shots and countered you to death. If you clutched and grappled, you paid with short body shots, uppercuts, and hooks.

"When you break Hagler down as a fighter, there is not one single thing not to like," says boxing writer and analyst Frank Lotierzo. "He was always in shape. He ate, drank and slept boxing. He had power. He could box. He could brawl. He had one of the best chins ever. If you love boxing, there's nothing negative you can say about Hagler."

To other fighters, Marvin was the complete package. Mustafa Hamsho, a durable fighter and legitimate contender, was another tough customer. Hamsho had emigrated from Syria to the US by himself at age fourteen by stowing away on a cargo ship. He had never been knocked down in thirty-two fights when he met Marvin for the first time in 1981. Hamsho was 32-1, his only loss coming in his first professional fight in 1975.

Trained by old nemesis Al Braverman, Hamsho took a bad beating that opened up two big cuts over both eyes and underneath one. In a post-fight interview, Marvin said he was hoping it would be stopped because "the meat from his eyes was hanging down." In fact, it was finally stopped in the eleventh and Marvin won by TKO.

"In my career, he was the only guy who hurt me. I fought everybody," Hamsho said in a rare interview in 2024. "He was a great fighter. He was sharp. He had a jab. He knew how to cut you."

They met again in 1984 at New York's Madison Square Garden, not far from the Brooklyn neighborhood where Hamsho grew up. The second fight was even more brutal as Marvin pounded Hamsho, knocking him down with a big right in the third that marked the first time he had been knocked down in his nine-year career. He stumbled to his feet but Marvin moved in and put him on the canvas again with an uppercut that put him flat on his back. Hamsho's trainer, Al Certo, saw his fighter was hurt, leaped into the ring, and stopped the fight.

"He was faster,"' Hamsho says. "I was a young guy. I was thinking nobody could hurt me in my life. Nobody could hurt me but him."

Marvin also had Goody in his corner—an underrated tactician, an expert cutman, a calming cornerman and friend, and a tireless workout partner who pushed Marvin daily to be the best in the sport.

"Goody was old school. He fought in the Navy and he had a good amateur career. He was taught how to box when boxing was at its peak, so he could impart the proper lessons on Hagler," Carlos Acevedo says. "He wasn't a genius. But he did take Hagler from teenager to legend and you can't underestimate that. People think of him as small-time but he produced a great fighter."

Tris Dixon says Marvin's back-to-basics training methods—including roadwork, simple resistance and strength training, stretching, and subjecting himself to extreme weather—toughened him up and worked in his favor.

"There are these haunting images of him training in Cape Cod in the snowy conditions. Horrifically cold, sparse conditions," he says. "Today, they train in heated gyms and luxury fitness clubs. You think about how basic and primitive Marvin's training was. It's astonishing."

There was something else: Marvin loved to have a good time, but he steered clear of drugs, booze, women, and shady characters for much of his career. Other fighters from his era such as Sugar Ray Leonard, Leon Spinks, and others fell into some of those traps, resulting in unwelcome distractions that affected their careers.

Fight promoter and film/TV producer Lou DiBella grew up watching Marvin fight. They became friends later in life and DiBella got to know Marvin, the man, not the fighter.

"Marvin was cool. Marvin didn't have to say anything to be cool." DiBella says. "Marvin had charisma."

Being a young Italian kid entering the fight game, DiBella got to know the Petronelli brothers and learned intimately why they had so much success as a "triangle" together with Marvin.

"It's almost love. It's almost familial," he said of their relationship. "They believed in Marvin. Marvin believed in them. They became family."

He compared their partnership to some of the most iconic relationships in boxing history—Cus D'Amato and Mike Tyson, Angelo Dundee and Muhammad Ali, Lou Duva and Pernell Whittaker, and Eddie Futch and Joe Frazier.

"Relationships make boxing. Always have," DiBella said. "It's equally important there's a trust level and a confidence level between fighter and trainer."

DiBella moved to Boston in 1978 and attended both Tufts University and Harvard Law School. The city, at the time, was mired in racial chaos as a federal judge ordered that schools be integrated, which sparked the Boston busing crisis that resulted in Black kids being pelted with rocks and subjected to disgraceful harassment while being bused to schools in white neighborhoods. The racial tension, much like similar clashes in Brooklyn, Newark, Watts, Detroit, and other cities, often pitted Italian immigrants against Blacks in a culture war that painted the Italians as angry racists.

The partnership between Marvin and the Petronellis was not only mutually beneficial, it was natural, and based on respect and commitment, which inspired Italians and young Blacks in Brockton, Boston, and beyond.

"People were getting bludgeoned with the poles of American flags over busing in Boston in the 1970s," DiBella recalls of the busing crisis. "The fact that he was embraced by Italians and became the pride of Boston, a working-class city that was all guineas, didn't hurt Marvin. The relationship with the Petronellis always helped Marvin. It helped him become an attraction."

In the Black community, too, Marvin's street cred was impeccable.

"To Black dudes, he was a motherfucker," DiBella says. "They said, 'This is our guy.' Marvin was his own man from beginning to end. He had universal respect in Beantown."

For Bob Arum, one of the biggest promoters in boxing history, what made Marvin special was his loyalty to the Petronelli brothers. He recalled a meeting with the brothers near Marvin's home in New Hampshire when they were trying to put together the Sugar Ray Leonard fight in 1986. Arum, Pat Petronelli, and Pat's wife, Betty, drove through a foggy night on the darkened highways of rural New Hampshire to meet with Marvin to talk about fighting Leonard.

Marvin was considering retiring and was not sure he would fight again, when the Petronelli brothers sought to sweeten the deal by taking a pay cut so Marvin could get a bigger share of the enormous purse. At the time, the fight was the most lucrative in the sport's history with Marvin being guaranteed $20 million and Leonard $13 million.

When Marvin learned of the brothers' offer to Arum to take a pay cut, Marvin went nuts.

"He was banging the table," Arum recalls. "Marvin looked at Pat and said, 'I don't give a damn. I don't know if I'm fighting that guy, but if I take the fight, you're taking your third and not a penny less. That told me without any doubt how tight the three of them were."

"You could always count on Marvin's loyalty," Arum added. "He expected you to be loyal to him. And his loyalty was ironclad. In this sport of boxing, fighters are influenced by outside people always buzzing in their ears. Marvin was not that way. If anyone ever went to him and talked to him about severing his relationship from Goody and Pat he would go crazy."

Arum said he built a strong relationship with Goody and Pat during the 1980s and described them as "stand-up guys."

"Pat and Goody Petronelli were two of the best people I've ever met in all the time I was in boxing," he said. "They were honest guys. They were hardworking. Marvin found his way to the gym that the Petronellis ran. He was a young kid. From that point on, he was with the Petronellis and he never, ever diverged from that. They were a real family. They were all tight; they were respectful of each other."

Their bond would be tested in the coming years, however, as Marvin battled his way up the ranks but was still being denied his title shot.

VINNIE CURTO

Marvin escaped his first three Philadelphia fights with a 1-2 record. Suitcase Sam Silverman and Rip Valenti convinced Russell Peltz to grant Marvin a rematch against Willie Monroe, this time in Boston. The fight took place on February 15, 1977, at the Hynes Convention Center.

The fight went differently this time. Marvin had learned.

Boston Herald boxing writer George Kimball described the fight in his book *The Four Kings*, writing:

"This time Hagler didn't leave it to the judges. In the final round of a twelve-round fight, Hagler caught Monroe with a right uppercut followed by a straight left and knocked him out cold."

It was a shot that showcased Marvin's raw punching power. It was so brutal that Goody from then on referred to Marvin's straight left as "The Willie Monroe Punch." Eddie Futch, who was Monroe's manager that night, was impressed.

"It seemed like every time we had Willie do something, Marvin did something else," he said.

Monroe blamed the loss on a cold.

"Two or three weeks before the fight, I fought in Rochester. I caught a cold," he said. "My manager made the fight with Marvin and I needed the money. I was confident. I figured I beat him the first time and I'd do it again."

"He was getting better and I was getting older," Monroe added. "He was in better condition. I had it won going into the twelfth round. But I was so tired and weak from the virus. He dropped me and the ref stopped it."

On the undercard that night was Vinnie Curto, an East Boston middleweight who had sparred with Marvin for years. Curto won his fight, earning him a shot at Marvin's New England title. That fight was set for September 24, 1977, but it never happened because of yet another strange chapter in boxing history.

Marvin fought two more times that summer—knocking out Reggie Ford and Roy Jones Sr., father of future star Roy Jones Jr.—and started training for his fight with Curto. A year younger than Marvin, Curto grew up in East Boston A year younger than Marvin, Curto grew up in East Boston and was molested and abused as a child.

"With a father who could only be called 'a monster,' I experienced things that would totally destroy most people," Curto wrote in a self-published memoir. "But ironically it was that monster who got me into boxing and paved the way for my first love . . . boxing."

Curto joined the US Navy, boxed amateur, and turned pro in Florida in 1972 under the guidance of Chris Dundee, Angelo Dundee's brother. Curto built a 24-4 record by 1977 when he was matched up with Marvin. In his memoir, he says that organized crime figures tried to force him to throw the fight but he refused and went on the run.

"I boxed a thousand rounds against him at the Petronelli's gym, and never lost one second," Curto said about Marvin. "Certain individuals wanted me to lay down in the first round, but I refused, asking them to let me fight."

He fled to Seattle and went underground for several months. The Massachusetts Commission suspended his license for skipping out on the fight. Lost and without income, he soon moved to Canada where he connected with none other than Frank Sinatra, who helped him get licensed to fight in the Great White North. Curto fought nine times in Montreal before getting his license back in the States.

"When I was in the dressing room in Montreal, after beating one of Canada's best, Eddie Melo, I got a wire from Sinatra congratulating me, and telling me I was reinstated in the US," Curto wrote.

Curto never fought Marvin. Many did not believe his Mob tale and thought he was simply afraid. After returning from Canada, Curto fought two more middleweight fights before moving up to super middleweight and light heavyweight.

One of his last middleweight fights was against Roger Phillips, a twenty-nine-year-old perpetual loser from Pittsfield, Massachusetts. Phillips was an illiterate alcoholic who was the divorced father of three kids from two different women. He was not a criminal but he spent many nights in the Pittsfield drunk tank.

He turned to boxing as a last-ditch effort to make something of his life, but his bout against Curto turned out to be his last. He took a bus to Portland, Maine, to fight Curto on March 6, 1981. It was a shameful matchup as Curto was the eleventh ranked middleweight in the world and Phillips was a tomato can with a 6-35 record who had lost twenty-four straight fights.

Not surprisingly, Curto punished him and the fight was stopped in the second round.

Phillips was paid $750 for the beating, one of the best paydays of his life, and he took the bus back to Pittsfield. The next day, he got drunk with his mother and bought himself some new clothes and bikes for his kids. He later went out partying and blew whatever cash he had left, leading to a violent altercation with his girlfriend. Police came to her house and arrested him.

Two days later, Phillips hanged himself in his jail cell.

Curto took the news hard but he had his own demons, notably the Mob. Over the ensuing years he led a turbulent life. He took a job as a security goon at the infamous Mustang Ranch, a mobbed-up brothel in Reno, and got involved with some characters, including Sammy "The Bull" Gravano. Through the years, he was shot and stabbed and his car was blown up in a failed assassination attempt.

In the eighties, the handsome, mustachioed fighter became an actor and appeared on Don Johnson's hit show, *Miami Vice*. He befriended Sylvester Stallone, who trained him during a short-lived boxing comeback. A movie about Curto's life was in the works for several years, with Mark Wahlberg set to play him and Robert DeNiro attached to portray Angelo Dundee, but it never happened. Curto's last fight was in 1996.

While Curto was on the run, he was replaced by undefeated Ray Phillips, who Marvin defeated by seventh-round TKO at Boston Garden, running Marvin's record to 34-2.

Just a few weeks before the fight, tragedy struck Marvin's camp. Suitcase Sam was killed when his blue Cadillac careened off of Route 2 in Cambridge, Massachusetts, struck another car and a fire hydrant and slammed into a utility pole. He was sixty-four.

Silverman was on his way home from a fight in upstate New York when the crash happened around 6:30 a.m. on July 9, 1977. The *Boston Globe* reported on the fatal wreck and mentioned that Silverman had been "shot at, bombed out, slugged and indicted" during his forty-plus years in boxing.

"There's nobody who can take Sam's place," Rip Valenti told the paper. "I know I'm certainly not about to do what he did and I don't know who will. He worked twenty-four hours a day on boxing."

There was speculation he may have had a heart attack behind the wheel, but Valenti said his friend "had a habit of driving fast."

"He was probably just in a hurry to get home and got sleepy or something behind the wheel," Valenti said.

The papers recalled him as a "cigar-chomping" Runyonesque character. He had no interest in other sports and recoiled when friends brought up the Red Sox, Celtics, or Bruins. Whenever talk of Bobby Orr, Ted Williams, or Bill Russell came up, Silverman turned the conversation to Ali, Frazier, Rocky, and Liston.

"He'd interrupt us and start talking about boxing," Valenti said. "That's all he knew and all he was interested in."

He promoted thirty-two of Rocky's forty-nine fights and was the matchmaker for twenty-five world-title fights. At the time of his death, he was in the middle of a lawsuit with the City of Boston over unpaid taxes.

Noted *Baltimore Sun* boxing writer Al Goldstein paid tribute to Silverman and wrote about his controversial side, which included allegations of fight-fixing, tax evasion, and FBI racketeering probes.

"These people just don't know Sam," his wife, Helen, a former showgirl, told Goldstein. "I could tell you about my miscarriage in 1953. Sam comes into the hospital and the first thing he says is, 'Helen, how do you suppose a Tommy Collins–Jimmy Carter fight would sell?' Not one word about feeling bad about the baby we lost."

"It's funny now, but it wasn't then," she continued. "But I learned something that night. Boxing was more important to Sam than anything. It was something sacred to him. Does that sound like someone who would fix a fight?"

Goldstein ended his compelling piece with a quote from old friend, Al Braverman: "There ain't no more Sam Silvermans in boxing."

"It was the perfect eulogy," Goldstein said.

For Marvin, Goody, and Pat, it was the end of an era. They were now left with Rip Valenti to do their bidding against Don King and Bob Arum.

It was all becoming too much for Marvin and Bertha as they struggled to get ahead. Marvin needed a title shot. Without Suitcase Sam around, it was more remote than ever.

A month after Silverman died, Marvin returned to The Spectrum for his third fight against Willie Monroe. This time, Marvin knocked him out in the second round.

"That was the fight that made him," Peltz said. "There was a complete difference between the Marvin that had fought in 1976 and 1977. The competition here had made him better. He had more confidence. He was sharper, his punches were shorter, he had more power."

Monroe fought just seven more times in his career, losing four. In his final fight, he was knocked out in the fourth round at Cobo Hall in Detroit by Motor City fighter Willie Sandman Edwards.

After retiring in 1981, Monroe refereed amateur bouts in Philadelphia and took a job working as a truck driver for the *Philadelphia Inquirer*, a job he continued until 2011. He had two daughters, one of whom became a Philadelphia police officer, and four grandchildren.

"He was a good guy, real quiet," his *Inquirer* boss, Pat McElwee, said. "But I wouldn't want to pick a fight with him."

Monroe died of Alzheimer's at home in 2019, surrounded by family. He was seventy-three.

Having beaten three of Philadelphia's four best middleweights, Marvin faced a pair of battles, one against Irish warrior Kevin Finnegan and the other a date at the Spectrum against "Bad" Bennie Briscoe.

But first, Marvin faced an even bigger battle outside the ring—one that pitted him against Don King.

CORRUPTION, SCANDAL, AND DON KING

In 1977, Don King was fresh off promoting the "Rumble in the Jungle" and the "Thrilla in Manilla"—two of the biggest fights in boxing history—which put him on the map as arguably the biggest promoter in the sport.

ABC and *The Ring* magazine, meanwhile, were seeking to cash in on the popularity of boxing in the wake of the Academy-Award-winning *Rocky*, as well as the success of US boxers in the Olympics in Montreal that year. The country was riding the patriotism of its Bicentennial celebration, so King created the "United States Boxing Championships," which quickly fell into scandal.

Through the years, countless boxers and promoters accused King of graft, strong-arming, corruption, and theft. He had long been accused of exploiting desperate and often uneducated Black fighters and bribing officials but always denied the accusations.

"I never got a fighter because I'm Black," King once said. "Every fighter . . . came to me after they've been screwed by other promoters."

But the truth is, King was a convicted criminal who once beat a man to death. He was the fifth of six kids, born in 1931 in Cleveland. His father, Clarence, was killed in a steel-plant explosion when King was just ten.

His mother moved them to a middle-class Ohio neighborhood with the insurance money from her husband's death and sold pies and roasted peanuts for a living. King, however, ventured down a darker path. After a failed stint at Case Western Reserve University, he became a bookie who ran illegal street lotteries in Cleveland, eventually earning the nickname "The King of Numbers."

In 1954, he shot and killed a man who tried to rob one of his gambling businesses. But he avoided jail because the act was ruled a justifiable homicide. King shot the victim in the back. A decade later, in 1967, he was found guilty of voluntary manslaughter for the beating death of thirty-four-year-old Sam Garrett, a Cleveland man who owed King six-hundred dollars. Witnesses said King stomped Garrett's head and pistol-whipped him. King served nearly four years in Marion Correctional Institution in Ohio for the killing and, after he was released in 1971, chose a life in boxing rather than on the streets. A year later, with the help of noted local promoter Don Elbaum, he convinced Ali to fight a charity bout in Cleveland.

In 1977, riding high from the two iconic heavyweight prizefights, he launched the United States Boxing Championships on ABC, with host Howard Cosell. The tournament was announced in January 1976 with typical King fanfare—from a boxing ring set up on the flight deck of the US Navy aircraft carrier the USS Lexington. ABC Sports president Roone Arledge, an attorney from Queens who was the same age as King, partnered with him to create the tournament. Arledge would later be known for creating *Monday Night Football, Nightline, 20/20,* and *ABC World News Tonight,* among other shows.

The fighters would be chosen from the rankings in *The Ring* magazine. But when the matchups for the televised tournament were announced, it was filled with mediocre fighters who left observers perplexed. Not surprisingly, most of the participants were fighters under contract with King.

King had already tried to get Marvin into his stable but Marvin rejected his advances, telling him that Goody and Pat were his team and that it was nonnegotiable. That did not help Marvin's chances at getting a title shot and it certainly played a role in him not being chosen for the ABC tournament. It would end up being a blessing in several ways.

Goody, Pat, and Marvin were outraged when they learned Marvin was blacklisted from the tournament. Some of the fighters in King's round-robin were guys Marvin had already beaten, including Willie Monroe and Johnny Baldwin.

"They neglected me," Marvin said. "I'm too good for my own good."

Marvin, Goody, and Pat were not the only ones who smelled a rat. So did Malcolm "Flash" Gordon, a twenty-seven-year-old underground writer from Queens peddling boxing newsletters outside major fights. Flash was dismissed as a renegade and called names like "sewer mongrel" and "beatnik pothead with body odor" by the boxing establishment. Gordon had already been breaking a good amount of boxing news in his guerrilla publication, *Flash Gordon's Tonight's Boxing Program and Weekly Newsletter*, which he handed out on the streets outside Madison Square Garden.

Gordon was known for bashing Arum and King, exposing corruption in the sport, and providing analysis that went beyond the ring and into bank accounts and boardrooms. His muckraking prompted boxing writer Bert Sugar to call him "the greatest anti-antihero boxing ever had."

Gordon looked at the tournament participant list and cross-referenced the fighters' managers with King's list of fighters. Not shockingly, nearly all were King fighters, many of whom had abruptly signed with the promoter shortly before the tournament was announced. Gordon also scrutinized *The Ring* magazine rankings. Again, not shockingly, many of the fighters who made it into the tournament made sudden appearances in *The Ring*'s rankings or jumped up several spots without any real justification.

A young producer at ABC Sports, Alex Wallau, was also suspicious of the tournament's list of fighters. ABC executives were alerted to the controversy and sought to tamp it down, calling in King, *Ring* magazine executives, and ABC Sports producers to give affidavits confirming the legitimacy of the tournament.

With those in hand, the tournament launched with Howard Cosell hosting. It did not take long until it all fell apart. Gordon started writing stories, pointing out the chicanery. The mainstream press soon picked up on it and a full-scale investigation was launched, filled with allegations of kickbacks, fraud, and bribes.

The Ring had inflated participants' records—in several cases fabricating victories for fights that never happened. King paid off the magazine's editor with $5,000 in cash and several boxers said King forced them to sign an exclusive promotion deal—just like the one that Marvin and the Petronelli brothers refused. Marvin and the Petronellis also refused a requirement to hire King's friends, Al Braverman and Paddy Flood, as Marvin's managers, while many other fighters in the tournament did.

In one glaring example, former middleweight journeyman Ike Fluellen, who was not active and was working as a cop in Texas, was suddenly ranked number ten in *The Ring*'s rankings. After signing an exclusive deal with King, he was credited with two phantom wins in Mexico. A few months later, without having a fight, *The Ring* rated him the number-three middleweight contender.

In all, investigators found that eleven of the sixty fighters in the tournament had records that were falsified, all of whom fraudulently rose up *The Ring*'s rankings. The scandal exploded after the Scott LeDoux–Johnny Boudreaux heavyweight fight. After losing a questionable decision, LeDoux crashed Boudreaux's post-fight interview with Cosell. A scuffle broke out during which Cosell's toupee was knocked off his head on live TV.

LeDoux, unlike most of the fighters in the tournament, was not signed to King. He later told Cosell that the tournament was fixed, much like professional wrestling, and that he was told to throw the fight. CBS' Dan Rather was working on a piece about King at the time and his crew caught the toupee incident on film. Rather aired it to show the sensationalism and shadiness permeating the sport.

Other press seized on ABC and *The Ring*, and soon a corruption probe was underway. While Marvin battled through the legitimate rankings,

ABC and *The Ring* scrambled for cover. *The Ring* magazine editors denied rigging the rankings and blamed the fiasco on shoddy recordkeeping. A grand jury in Baltimore began hearing evidence about kickbacks and fraud.

Still, King would not quit. He was determined to maximize promotion, regardless of the tournament's validity. He took his sideshow to Marion Correctional Facility, where he had done four years in prison for manslaughter a few years before. It was March 6, 1977, and he broadcast a ninety-minute live boxing card that was the first live TV event ever broadcast from inside a US prison. Meanwhile, the FBI and IRS investigations carried on beyond the prison walls.

Cosell hosted the broadcast while Joe Louis provided color commentary ringside. The audience was made up of fourteen hundred inmates, a few dignitaries, and some media. King grabbed the mic in the center of the ring and bloviated.

"I look around and see many familiar faces," King told the crowd. "I am one of you."

"It is with mixed emotions that I am coming back to what was trauma in my life," he continued. "I am happy and proud to be able to bring back some entertainment for you because you have been part of my life."

Inmates chided Cosell. One sign read: "Howard got in—will he get out?" Another read: "Finally, Howard is where he belongs."

King hammed it up with the inmates, celebrating his felonious past and treating the event like a university homecoming.

"Wherever I have gone outside, I have never tried to hide Marion C.I. I never forget No. 125734," he said, reciting his inmate number.

A month later, as the scandal blew up in the press, ABC pulled the plug on the tournament. The curtain fell on King's caper in April 1977, just before a bout that was scheduled between future heavyweight champion Larry

Holmes, who was then 24-0 and ranked fourth in the world, and Stan Ward, who was 8-0 and ranked eighth.

Several fighters were credited with wins they either never earned or for fights that never actually happened, including:

- Lightweight Pat Dolan—four fake 1975 wins in New York and New Jersey.
- Featherweight Hilbert Stevenson—five wins and a draw in 1976.
- Junior Middleweight Anthony House—seven wins and a draw in 1975 and three in 1976.
- Junior Middleweight Mel Dennis of Houston—two fake knockouts in Argentina in 1976.

Also, Floyd Mayweather Sr., father of future star Floyd Mayweather Jr., was credited with fake wins in 1975 and 1976. Mayweather's reward for the scandal was a 1978 fight against Sugar Ray Leonard in which Mayweather Sr. broke his hand and was knocked out. Mayweather Sr. was famously shot in the leg four months later—while holding his future-champion son in his arms—which seriously injured his leg and effectively ended his fight career. Mayweather Sr. later spent five and a half years in federal prison in the 1990s for cocaine trafficking and started training his son after his release.

There were investigations into the ABC/*Ring* scandal by the FBI and IRS. At the same time, *Sports Illustrated* and other media outlets probed whether their writers were paid to give the tournament favorable coverage and boost the phony rankings.

No criminal charges were ever filed but the scandal shook the sport. New York State Boxing Commissioner James A. Farley Jr., who sanctioned the tournament, was forced to resign.

ABC issued a mea culpa, which read: "ABC has now determined that the records of numerous fighters in the tournament as listed in the 1977 *Ring* [record] book are, in fact, inaccurate and contain many fights which apparently never took place."

A September 1977 report commissioned by ABC found "a good deal of unethical behavior by individuals involved with the administration and organization of the tournament." The FCC gave ABC a slap on the wrist, formally admonishing the network for "negligence and careless conduct," but issued no formal sanctions.

King vented his anger over the scandal by suspending Braverman and Flood, as well as his PR man Gordon Peterson. He also blamed racism for the scrutiny of the tournament.

"With all these rumors, there's smoke, and where there's smoke there's usually fire," he said. But, he added, the investigation was an attempt to "fry this coon."

Notably, Muhammad Ali came to King's support, saying: "There's only one thing wrong. They got a spook running the tournament."

Flash Gordon continued publishing his newsletter for several more years but fell into obscurity. He is believed to have died in 2017.

King of course went on to promote some of the biggest fights in the eighties and nineties and control the career of Mike Tyson. But he never gained control over Marvin—and, in fact, he would soon face a pair of political heavyweights who came to Marvin's aid.

STRENGTHENING "THE TRIANGLE"

While the ABC scandal unfolded, the boxing world started to recognize Marvin's talent. In Philadelphia, Marvin ran into Joe Frazier and complained that he was being blackballed.

"I can't get no fights," he told Frazier.

The champ, who had watched Marvin run through some of the best fighters in his gym, famously told Marvin: "You have three strikes against you—you're Black, you're a southpaw, and you're good."

Fighters ducked Marvin and promoters avoided him. Whether the rigged ABC tournament was designed specifically to keep Marvin out is debatable. It was certainly convenient to not have Marvin in it, and beneficial to King to not have a fighter not under his control in the tournament, knocking his guys out of it and possibly unconscious. Either way, it was all skulduggery and Marvin was collateral damage.

He remained an outsider. Before he could get a title shot—rigged rankings or not—he had to go through Kevin Finnegan, Bennie Briscoe, and Mike Colbert, all of whom were tough, well-trained, and eager to take out Marvin.

First up was the division's number-one contender, Colbert, in November 1977, at Boston Garden. From Portland, Oregon, Colbert was 22-0. A few months earlier, in April 1977, Colbert won a split decision over twenty-seven-year-old Rocky Mosely Jr. in Miami. A year earlier, he knocked out Mosely's forty-one-year-old father, Rocky Mosely Sr., which made Colbert only the second fighter in history to beat a father and son. It did not matter to Marvin.

Colbert's nickname was "The Cobra," which prompted Marvin to call himself "The Mongoose."

"You know what a mongoose does?" Hagler asked the press. "It destroys cobras."

Before a crowd of 3,800 at the Garden, Colbert ran from Hagler for most of the fight until the end of the eleventh round when Marvin caught him with a big right that broke his jaw.

"I heard something snap," Colbert later recalled.

Wounded, Colbert came out for the eleventh to a barrage. In his maroon velour shorts, Marvin surged forward, his tight, sharp punches pounding Colbert's face. Marvin drove him into the ropes and hit him with a cold-blooded combination that knocked down Colbert and broke his jaw on the other side.

Colbert somehow got to his feet and stood for an eight-count before Marvin moved back in and finished him off with four shots that dropped Colbert back to the canvas. His bloody mouthpiece fell out of his mouth as he took the full count on his hands and knees. Marvin had the biggest KO of his career to that point.

"A man sooner or later has to run out of gas and there is no place for a refill in the ring with me," Marvin said after the fight. "I was looking for a mistake. And he made it."

Colbert's trainer, Mike Morton, later falsely claimed that Marvin broke Colbert's jaw with a punch thrown after the bell rang to end round eleven. Colbert was humble in defeat.

"Hagler gave me a good whuppin'. I have no complaints," he said.

Colbert went to Mass General where his broken jaw was wired shut. It was broken in three places. Colbert was one of several opponents Marvin sent from the Garden to the nearby Boston hospital.

A month after the loss, Colbert announced his retirement, saying he was enrolling at Oregon State University to pursue an electrical engineering degree.

"I want to get my education," he said. "The only reason I was ever in boxing in the first place was to make enough money to quit and go to school."

His retirement was short-lived, however. He returned to the ring and had a dozen fights over the next three years, including a draw with Sugar Ray Seales in Seattle in 1979, and a decision loss to Thomas Hearns in New Orleans five months later. After 1981 he fought just twice before he retired for good in 1986, when he changed his name to Adolfo Akil and became an accountant.

Marvin trained for the fight at the Provincetown Inn, putting himself into full isolation in the town at the very tip of Cape Cod, far from Brockton. Provincetown, which in those days was largely desolate except in summer months, became his boxing sanctuary. It was there that he reflected on his career and brooded about being overlooked by the boxing system.

Goody and Marvin ran miles in the cold sands of the frigid Provincetown winter, the icy ocean lapping up against the beach as they ran side-by-side, exhaling steam into the bitter cold.

Pat worked the phones while Marvin and Goody went rounds simulating fights to prepare for the slate of middleweights in front of Marvin. While still considered a small fish in Vegas and Atlantic City, Pat was no pushover. He fought for his fighter and made sure that the Triangle was protected.

"He went toe-to-toe with promoters, lawyers, other managers and trainers, television officials, referees, and all comers who dared to be less than fair to any of his fighters," friend Tony DeMarco once said of Pat. "He was known as a tough negotiator with a heart soft as putty. He never failed to come to the aid of family, friends, and boxers who needed help—whether it was a tank of fuel, an uninsured medical expense, or a stint in a rehab."

Inside the ring, Goody flourished as a tactician. While pushing sixty he was a natural trainer who could mimic the moves of Finnegan, Colbert, Briscoe, and the rest, challenging Marvin to adjust his style to take advantage of vulnerabilities and openings. They were developing a rare rhythm and knew what the other was about to do before it happened.

"Whatever Pat brought to the table it worked. Pat had an air of honesty and loyalty. You'll never find a triangle like Goody, Pat, and Marvin," said Al Valenti, grandson of Rip. "[They] were honest with one another. [Marvin] could have ended up with Vinnie Vecchione. But he ended up with Goody and Pat."

Tony Petronelli also witnessed the dynamic.

"My uncle Goody was in the service, so everything was 'yes sir, no sir,'" Tony said. "My father, he had the gift of gab. He could talk you out of anything. And Marvin did the fighting. My father did the talking. My uncle Goody did the keeping in shape. It worked."

Bertha and the kids were mostly barred from camp, but visited on occasion. She was no longer allowed to sit ringside and work the bell, but it was always a welcome reprieve for Marvin to see his wife and hold his kids for a few minutes. He was laser-focused but being a father was always a priority for Marvin.

Marvin, like Goody, also was meticulous about his health. He ate a rigid high-protein diet created by Goody, slept on a schedule, and kept a military-like routine. He called training "prison," choosing the remote Provincetown Inn to eliminate distractions.

Marvin liked the isolation of Provincetown. He knew he was not a media favorite like Sugar Ray Leonard or Muhammad Ali. He knew he had to outwork everyone and leave nothing to chance if he wanted to become a world champion.

Goody and Pat were also outsiders. They were blue-collar, small-town trainers. They had some success with Tony Petronelli but with Marvin they were inching closer to the sport's apex. To the boxing elite, they were not on the level of Eddie Futch, Angelo Dundee, and Ray Arcel. But, as with Marvin, disrespect drove them.

By 1977, they knew they had a champion in Marvin and they were going to do everything in their power to prove it. The shared underdog mentality made their bond strong.

"My father and Goody didn't just have a champion," Tony Petronelli says. "They had a superstar in Marvin."

Goody knew Marvin's enormous upside.

"Pat and I could see we had a potential world champion on our hands, but we still had a big mountain to climb," Goody said.

After beating Colbert, next up was Finnegan, who four months before had lost a decision to Alan Minter at Wembley Arena. Rip Valenti brought Finnegan to fight Marvin at Boston Garden on March 3, 1978.

Against the rugged Finnegan, Marvin was masterful. He landed combinations at will over eight rounds. He opened four cuts that resulted in the fight being stopped. Like Colbert, Finnegan ended his night getting stitches at Mass General.

Two months later, Marvin fought Finnegan again, scoring a seventh-round TKO at Boston Garden. Despite the beatings, Finnegan never got knocked down. Marvin later said Finnegan was his toughest opponent.

National Front propaganda flyer circa 1977.

Fight poster for the middleweight title fight between Marvin and Alan Minter on September 27, 1980.

The press, including this British newspaper, reported broadly about Alan's racist pre-fight comment about Marvin.

Ticket to the title fight between Marvin and Alan Minter at Wembley Arena on September 27, 1980.

Marvin collapses to his knees after defeating Alan in the third round.
Getty Images

Goody, Pat, Steve Wainright, Marvin's brother Robbie Sims, and others protect Marvin from bottles raining down on the ring from angry drunken fans. *Courtesy of John Merian Jr.*

Marvin's hometown newspaper declares that he is the world champion. *Courtesy of John Merian*

The Triangle—and Marvin is world champion. *Courtesy of Artie Dias*

Marvin's mother Ida Mae speaks with Brockton Mayor Rober F. Sullivan at a memorial service for Marvin following his March 13, 2021 death. *Photo by author*

Among the mourners at the service was Thomas Hearns, Marvin's opponent in "The War," one of the most thrilling firefights in boxing history.
Photo by author

The City of Brockton named a new street Marvelous Marvin Hagler Way in the champion's honor in 2021.
Photo by author

A bronze statue in Marvin's honor was dedicated in the new Marvelous Marvin Hagler Park, next to the site of the former Petronelli Gym, in 2024. *Photo by author*

BACK TO THE SPECTRUM

The victories set up Marvin's return to the Spectrum. But this time was different—he was known and no longer needed Philadelphia as a proving ground. He was the fighter to beat.

Bennie Briscoe was the last of the four Philadelphia fighters Marvin had to go through, after already facing Cyclone Hart, Willie Monroe, and Boogaloo Watts. Like all the others, Briscoe was a tough out. He was 60-15-5 coming into the fight.

Also like several Philadelphia fighters, Briscoe was a transplant. Born in 1943 in Augusta, Georgia, he was one of fourteen kids and grew up poor. He was a standout football player and track athlete. He once caddied for President Dwight D. Eisenhower at Augusta National Golf Club.

He moved to North Philadelphia when he was sixteen to live with two aunts and attended Simon Gratz High School. It was there that he wandered into Joe Frazier's gym and began training alongside the future heavyweight champion. During the day, he was a city worker, first on the rat patrol and later as a garbage man. Throughout his life, wherever he was, he sent money from his weekly paycheck back to his mother in Georgia.

"If he had a million dollars, he wouldn't have a dime," Briscoe's brother Archie once said. "He would give it all away. He knew what it was like to be hungry."

Briscoe started fighting pro in 1962. In 1967, he fought Carlos Monzon before Monzon won the title. The fight was in Buenos Aires in Monzon's homeland of Argentina and Briscoe gave the favorite all he could handle. The fight was scored a draw but many thought Briscoe won.

A few years later, in 1972, when Monzon was the undisputed middleweight champion, he gave Briscoe a shot at the title, again in Argentina. It was another battle, as Monzon was seriously hurt by an overhand right in the ninth that spun him and left him dazed. Monzon clinched to clear his head and eventually battled back to win a fifteen-round decision.

In 1974, Briscoe fought for the vacant WBC middleweight title in Monaco, losing by seventh-round TKO to Rodrigo Valdes. He also fought former world champion Emile Griffith twice. In their first meeting in 1974, Briscoe lost a close decision at the Spectrum. In 1976, he fought Griffith to a draw in Monaco.

"When Bennie fights, he comes to fight, he don't come to play," Griffith said.

Russell Peltz promoted the August 24, 1978, Briscoe–Hagler fight in Philadelphia and recalls a meeting with Goody and Pat, during which they expressed frustration that they could not get Marvin a title shot. The brothers asked Peltz if he wanted to join their team and own a piece of Marvin. But Peltz—with Marvin's losses to Monroe and Watts fresh in his mind—declined. It's a decision that haunted him for decades.

"They cornered me outside my locker room," Peltz remembers. "They offered me a piece of the fighter at no cost."

"We'll cut you in," Pat told him.

But Peltz was focused on his Philadelphia stable and passed up the offer.

"That's how I turned down 10 percent of Marvelous Marvin Hagler," he says. "If I'd been smarter, I'd have signed him. But we didn't just think that way in those days."

Peltz would often comp his fighters' meals. It turned out to be an expensive proposition when it came to Marvin, whose large entourage, mostly made up of family, ran up huge tabs.

"Hagler started bringing family with him and we started getting these rather high meal bills," Peltz remembers.

Attorney Steve Wainwright was part of his entourage. A flamboyant, bald-headed barrister, Wainwright was the son of former Brockton Mayor Richard Wainwright and was from a well-connected family of lawyers. He wore sparkly satin coats emblazoned with the word "BARRISTER" in rhinestones, sunglasses indoors and out, was friends with actress Bo Derek, and provided a lot of flash—and legal muscle—to Marvin's entourage.

"He was worth the price of admission to take a meeting with him because he was such a unique character and a bit of a nut," said George Krieger, former vice president of HBO Sports. "They should have made a TV series about him."

It was Wainwright, a few years later, who filed the paperwork for Marvin to legally change his name to "Marvelous Marvin Hagler." Marvin made the name change in 1982 to thwart the media, ring announcers, and anyone else who refused to use his "Marvelous" ring name. To him, it was maddening that announcers would refer to Joe Frazier as "Smokin' Joe," or Ray Leonard as "Sugar," but would not say "Marvelous." So changing his name legally precluded anyone from ever disrespecting him again.

The press called the Briscoe fight the "The Battle of the Balds" because both fighters sported clean-shaven heads. The Spectrum was packed that night with more than fourteen thousand fans. To this day, it was the biggest nontitle fight crowd in Philadelphia history.

There was also an interesting side story to the fight, as Peltz nearly booked an undercard exhibition match that would have pitted outspoken Philadelphia

City Councilor Francis Rafferty—who boxed amateur in the US Army—against Black activist Milton Street. The two nearly fought on the floor of the Philadelphia City Council a few weeks before the fight over a proposal to end term limits for the city's mayor. During the dustup, Rafferty called Street a "faggot," which prompted Street to call the councilor a "racist." But the state boxing commission blocked the novelty bout, robbing Peltz of a few headlines.

It turned out that the main event was all anyone needed.

Marvin again locked down in Provincetown to train. He had six different sparring partners, including Tiger Moore, and swapped them in and out to simulate different styles that Briscoe might use. He and Goody ran their miles in the hot August sand out on Race Point on the tip of Cape Cod.

"All I do when I'm running is dream," Marvin said. "I dream of being the champion . . . All I want is a shot. Give me a shot."

Goody continued to talk up his fighter to the press every chance he got. He knew Marvin was ready to beat anyone who came along.

"Marvin is the most feared fighter in the world today," Goody said.

In another interview, Marvin predicted he would send Briscoe, then thirty-five, into retirement.

"This is the fight I've been waiting for," Marvin said. "I want that man bad."

Briscoe, meanwhile, was confident. He had a tradition of calling his mother immediately after he won a fight. He predicted he would be dialing her number in Georgia shortly after the final bell at The Spectrum.

"I can't wait till it's all over," he said. "Then I can call my mother and tell her I won again."

Marvin countered: "This is Bennie's last hurrah and he knows it. I want to dispose of him in front of his people."

With Wainwright backing up Pat on the business side, Marvin was paid $17,500 for the bout, which was also broadcast live via closed-circuit TV at Boston Garden, thanks to Rip Valenti. The fight was the largest gate at The Spectrum at the time, proving that Marvin was not only a legitimate contender, but also a box-office draw. The sport's power brokers were starting to take notice.

Tickets were just seven, ten, and fifteen dollars and fans got more than their money's worth. The two men were as advertised, showing why they were widely known as two of the division's hardest punchers.

In the second round, Marvin rocked Briscoe with a straight right, bloodying Briscoe's nose and knocking him sideways. In the third, Marvin was cut along his right eye, from what appeared to be a headbutt. Blood poured down Marvin's face and there were concerns from his corner that the fight could be stopped if the cut was not closed.

Goody went to work.

"I'm not sure what coagulant he used but I'm pretty sure it was illegal," said author and fight analyst Carlos Acevedo.

"I felt the coldness coming down my eye," Marvin said of the gash. "I got my confidence back by taking care of the fight and letting my trainer take care of my eye."

Briscoe had a great seventh round, but Marvin won the later rounds and took home a unanimous decision. The victory ran Marvin's record to 41-2-1 with 33 KOs and elevated him to the eighth-ranked middleweight in the world. It also inched him closer to a title shot, but there would be more work to do.

One person who was sure of Marvin's greatness was Briscoe's trainer, George Benton, whose nickname in the boxing world was "The Professor."

"This guy will beat the champ. This guy can beat anybody," Benton said.

The Philadelphia press, too, left no doubt as to Marvin's performance. The rarely understated *Philadelphia Daily News* plastered the sports page with a headline that read: "HAGLER HUMILIATES AN OLD HERO." Boxing writer Thom Greer, meanwhile, called it a "boxing clinic" and said the decision was "a gross understatement."

"Bennie Briscoe was totally outclassed," Greer wrote.

Briscoe went on to fight thirteen more times, losing seven. He remained a humble, dedicated city worker in the Philadelphia sanitation department until he died in 2010 at sixty-seven.

In one of his last interviews, he said: "Other guys that started out when I started out, they're either in jail or on drugs, or they're dead, and I'm still here. I love my mother and my father, and that's why I think I lasted so long."

The victory was sweet for Marvin and ran his record at the dreaded Spectrum to 3-2, with victories over Briscoe, Willie Monroe, and Cyclone Hart. His work with Goody and Pat, his tenacity, and his willingness to fight anyone and beat them convincingly left little doubt that he was the best middleweight in the world, or at least worthy of a shot at proving it.

There were still many obstacles ahead, including a shot at revenge for the Boogaloo Watts decision. But most of all, he wanted respect and a chance to fight for the belts that so many thought he deserved.

CONGRESSIONAL INTERVENTION

After disposing of Benny Briscoe, Marvin returned to Boston Garden on the undercard of a fight between Vito Antuofermo and "Irish" Mike Hallacy. Vito was 43-3 and won a unanimous decision.

Marvin fought Willie Warren, a fighter from Corpus Christi, Texas, who had a record of 44-39. Marvin punished the Texan, who had no business being in the ring with Marvin. Warren refused to come out for the start of the seventh, giving Marvin the TKO victory.

After beating Warren, Marvin had a rubber match at Boston Garden against Sugar Ray Seales. This time, the two fighters were in different leagues. Marvin knocked Seales down three times in the first round and the fight was stopped. A month later, and again barely breaking a sweat, Marvin beat Bob Patterson by third-round TKO in Providence. Two months later, he beat Jamie Thomas at Cumberland County Civic Center in Portland, Maine, also by third-round TKO.

Meanwhile, the ABC/*Ring* scandal made it all the way to the desks of two of the most powerful politicians in the nation: US Senator Edward M. "Ted" Kennedy and US House Speaker Thomas P. "Tip" O'Neill, both of whom represented Massachusetts and knew Marvin and the Petronellis.

Many friends of Marvin and the brothers complained to Tip and Ted about the corrupt boxing world and begged them to step in to get Marvin the shot he deserved at a world title.

Ted had an affinity for Marvin after meeting him in Provincetown, which is a short ride from the Kennedy family compound, and Ted sometimes traveled down to watch Marvin train. Marvin in turn lent his campaign support to Ted over the years, including appearing at parades and fundraisers to support the senator.

O'Neill was a South Boston native who grew up loving boxing. He had great respect for the sport and Marvin's approach to it. Both lawmakers had enormous clout in Washington, DC, and were furious over the ABC/*Ring* scandal. Shortly after news of the rigged tournament exploded, Arum received two letters—one from Kennedy and another from O'Neill.

"Both letters said the same thing: it was an outrage that their constituent Marvin Hagler wasn't being given an opportunity to fight for the middleweight championship," Arum said. "They told me that if I didn't arrange sooner rather than later for Hagler to fight for the championship, there would be a joint committee investigation into boxing."

"My ass would go before a joint committee," Arum said. "I obviously realized I didn't need this problem."

As the scandal rocked the sport, the heat increased on Arum to give Marvin a shot—from a host of Washington heavyweights. In addition to pressure from O'Neill and Kennedy, Wainwright went to two of his Beltway connections: US Senator Paul Tsongas, of Lowell, Massachusetts, and US Representative Edward Beard of nearby Rhode Island. Both were big boxing fans.

Beard fired off a letter to WBC President Jose Sulaiman suggesting that "the WBC seemed to be stalling in giving Hagler his chance" and that "maybe it was time for a congressional investigation into boxing."

"Politicians love a fight," Pat Petronelli said as the pressure built to give Marvin a title shot. "And they really warmed up to this one."

Around the same time of Beard's letter, O'Neill's son, Thomas P. O'Neill III, says his father received a personal visit from Goody and Marvin at his Congressional office in Boston.

"I've seen every one of your fights," Tip told Marvin.

"My guy deserves a shot," Goody told him. "Arum is blocking him out."

According to O'Neill III, his father, who died in 1994, told his chief of staff to call Arum and demand a title shot for Marvin.

"Tell Bob Arum that if he doesn't give this kid a shot at the title within the calendar year, we're going to launch an investigation into the fight game," Tip O'Neill said.

The message was delivered and Arum heard it loud and clear. Arum knew the stakes of a federal probe into the sport. He wanted nothing to do with it, so he called Marvin's promoter, Rip Valenti.

"Rip, I got these letters, you gotta get these people off my ass," Arum said.

The press was starting to pick up Marvin's cause too. In late 1977, the *Associated Press* called him "the new Rocky." It was becoming clear to everyone in and around the sport—Goody and Pat, Bob Arum, Steve Wainwright, Don King, and especially the people of Brockton—that Marvin was indeed the heir to Marciano's throne. He would never be Rocky. Who could replace an undefeated legend? But he had that same aura of invincibility and underdog mentality that made you root for him.

Marvin and Rocky were different fighters, but had the same two qualities that set them apart—relentless commitment and heart. Marvin rarely talked about living in Rocky's shadow but was proud to be from the same city. He respected Rocky's achievements.

He and Goody sometimes talked about Rocky and what made him great. Goody shared training tips and secrets about Rocky's regimen and style that helped Marvin. He also reminded Marvin that he had many of the same qualities that made Rocky great.

"If you don't have a good chin, forget it," Goody said. "God supposedly created us all equal. He really didn't. He created some with chins, and some without."

"I never met Marciano myself," said Hagler, "but I feel as though I know the man. I love his techniques about training, how he'd put himself into 'jail.' And how all the odds were against him. . . . We have the same type of motives, to punish the body as far as the body can go, to go into the ring and get our jobs done."

They may have been from different backgrounds, but they had much in common. The greasy shoe shops of Brockton and dirt lots that raised Rocky were not that different from the bombed-out buildings and empty factories of Newark that gave Marvin his edge. Both paid their dues, fought with pride, took no shortcuts, and were honored to be representing the hardscrabble city of Brockton.

"He put Brockton on the map," Marvin once said. "It's my job to keep it there. It's a beautiful place."

Goody and Pat were extremely proud of both men. But while Rocky got his title shot early in his career, the brothers were still battling to get Marvin his after nearly fifty fights. They continued their political battles with the boxing establishment and turned to the press to ratchet up the pressure and help them get Marvin a title shot. The ABC/*Ring* scandal ended up working in Marvin's favor as many in the boxing world realized it was absurd that he was blackballed by King, Braverman, and their henchmen.

"There's still a lot of politics in boxing," Hagler told the AP. "It's who you know. But I'll get a title shot if I get one break."

When Marvin was asked about the scandal, he said: "I beat four guys King put in that tournament. The ratings don't mean nothing. It only counts when you're champion."

Marvin's knockouts and growing public persona had the Petronellis fielding calls from promoters, agents, managers, and others who wanted a piece of their young fighter. Offers came for Marvin to move to world-class training facilities with state-of-the-art equipment and trainers. Despite being one of the world's top contenders, he continued to train at the Petronelli Brothers Gym, which was plastered with yellowing, peeling boxing posters from the fifties and sixties, and had poor lighting, a single rusty shower, and a broken clock.

King and others came forward and tried to steal Marvin from the brothers. King appealed to Bertha, luring her with promises of riches, private jets, and swanky hotels. It nearly worked as Marvin and Bertha considered leaving the Petronellis. They were going to move to California and start over with new management.

Marvin went so far as to go to Goody and Pat to break the news.

"I can't wait any longer," he said.

"Marvin, you've got to keep winning to get a shot," Pat told him. "If you win this [next] one, Marvin, you've got it."

It was déjà vu for Marvin, however. He'd beaten fifty men in the ring—many of whom had their shot, some repeatedly.

"Every time I won, there was nothing," Marvin said. "Every day I was out there running, paving the ground, getting knocked around in the gym, keeping sharp, getting ready."

Goody and Pat begged him to stick it out with them a little longer.

"I'm not getting any younger," Marvin said.

"Look, if we felt as though we couldn't do it for you, we'd be the first ones to let you find something else," Goody told him.

"I gotta think about this," he said. "The rent has to be paid. The kids have to have clothes. There hasn't been nobody giving me nothin'!"

Goody and Pat certainly understood Marvin's struggle. They reminded him of the journey they had taken together, from that first day Marvin walked into the gym with holes in his shoes until that very moment, when they were teetering on the brink of superstardom.

"We came up the hard way. Anything we got we worked for. That's why there's a bond between us," Pat said.

"We were never given anything on a silver platter," Goody added.

Marvin wanted to trust them and put his faith in them. But he also was watching fighters like Sugar Ray Leonard rake in massive purses and endorsement deals that were still eluding him.

He sat with Bertha in their Brockton living room. They went over the possible scenarios. Moving to California with their young kids would be difficult. And what if he didn't have a fight for a year or more? What if he didn't get a title shot? At least he knew with Goody and Pat, he had a team he could trust.

Marvin, ultimately, believed in the Triangle.

"I'm going to stick with Goody and Pat," he told Bertha.

They unpacked their bags and decided to give it one last shot in Brockton with the Petronellis.

"It was tough," Marvin said of the decision.

The move paid off. Caving to the threats from the Massachusetts politicians, Arum called a meeting in New York with Goody and Pat, where he promised Marvin a shot.

"I said, 'Look, I don't want any problems,'" recalled Arum.

He promised to put Marvin on the undercard of the Vito Antuofermo–Hugo Corro middleweight championship fight in Monte Carlo.

"If he wins, I'll arrange for him to fight the winner," Arum told the brothers.

Corro was middleweight champion at the time and had not lost a fight in more than three years. Antuofermo, then twenty-six, came to the United States when he was fifteen. He was brought into a gym in Brooklyn by a local police officer and learned to box.

Marvin had been preparing to fight Antuofermo and Corro for years. He did not care who he fought anymore. He salivated at the thought of challenging either one for the belt.

VITO "THE MOSQUITO"

Antuofermo and Corro met on Saturday, June 30, 1979, at Chapiteau de l'Espace Fontvieille in Monaco. Marvin was on the undercard, matched against Norberto Rufino Cabrera, an Argentine fighter who was 22-7. Marvin was then the number-one contender in the world while Antuofermo was fifth. Alan Minter was ranked second, behind Marvin, while Cabrera was ninth.

Before the fight, Marvin used the press to taunt and shame the entire middleweight division.

"Why won't they fight me?" he asked reporters.

Cabrera had no business being in the ring with Marvin. In fact, no one was beating Marvin at this point—other than the judges. Marvin punished Cabrera, a former Olympian, over eight rounds before Cabrera's corner threw in the towel. The crowd included a strong American contingent that cheered wildly for Marvin after the victory, chanting "World champ!" over and over.

In his post-fight interview, Marvin kept up the bravado. Asked who he preferred to fight for the title, Antuofermo or Corro, Marvin said, "It wouldn't take me longer with either of them than it did with Cabrera."

Cabrera was stunned at the punishment he took.

"Hagler lands his blows faster than anything I've ever seen," Cabrera said. "Where I was expecting two or three blows, I'd get three or four. . . . He would beat Corro or Antuofermo in less than seven rounds."

Antuofermo took care of business, beating Corro via a split decision over fifteen rounds, to earn the title.

Arum said Corro and Antuofermo watched in awe at Marvin's easy destruction of Cabrera.

"People say that when Antuofermo and Corro fought each other, each of them was happy for the other guy to win. They didn't want to fight Marvin," Arum said.

After the fight, Arum was true to his word and set up a title fight between Marvin and Antuofermo at Caesars Palace in Vegas. The bout was set for just a few months later, on November 30, 1979.

Marvin had waited his whole life for the moment and reveled in it. He told press before the fight: "I see myself with my hands in the air and Vito down on his back."

"I hear the referee say, 'The new middleweight champion, Marvelous Marvin Hagler,'" he said.

Marvin handed out fly swatters to the press and said: "I'm gonna swat him down like a fly. I call him 'Vito the Mosquito.'" It was a nickname that would stick with Antuofermo for the rest of his career.

Marvin's old sparring partner Tony Petronelli fought on the undercard and won a unanimous decision. While it was a title fight, Hagler–Antuofermo was not the main event. That distinction went to Sugar Ray Leonard who took the WBC welterweight title from Wilfred Benitez via TKO.

In the co-feature to the Leonard–Benitez fight, Marvin and Vito squared off.

"Marvin was at his best over the first half of that fight," recalled boxing writer Michael Katz. "He was landing combinations, hitting Antuofermo with everything he threw. Only Vito's chin kept him in that fight."

Marvin seemed to have controlled the fight and most thought he was in command going into the twelfth. Marvin had never gone fifteen rounds but here he was, on boxing's biggest stage, against the middleweight champion of the world, pushing himself to go the distance.

Antuofermo fought desperately in the late rounds, knowing he was behind. In the final round, Antuofermo caught Marvin with an uppercut that rocked his head back and nearly knocked him down. But Marvin was never hurt and most in attendance agreed that he won most rounds and would be crowned the new champion.

After the final bell, referee Mills Lane approached Goody and Pat.

"Step aside, because when I raise Marvin's hand up I want them to take a picture of just him and me," Lane said.

But Marvin would get another education on bad decisions. When the scorecards were announced, it recalled the bogus Boogaloo Watts decision. Judge Duane Ford had it 145-141 in Hagler's favor. Dalby Shirley scored it 144-142 for Antuofermo while the third judge, Hal Miller, had it even at 143-143.

"Vito retains the title. Good lord, they called it a draw," announcer Howard Cosell said. "Hagler is absolutely disgusted."

Antuofermo, his face battered and swollen, was hoisted atop the shoulders of his cornermen and raised his arms in victory.

Marvin was devastated and quickly made his way out of the ring.

Joe Louis, who was sitting ringside in a wheelchair, reached up and grabbed Marvin's arm as he walked by.

"They stole it from you, champ," Louis whispered to him.

Marvin looked at him, expressionless.

"Hey kid, you won that fight," the Brown Bomber told him. "Don't give up."

"I'll be back in the gym tomorrow," Marvin replied.

Marvin was furious. So were Goody and Pat. Their guy had been robbed again. But this time it was not at the Spectrum in a tune-up fight. It was in Vegas for the world title.

"I thought Marvin won at least eight rounds and Vito no more than four," said Bob Arum.

Tip O'Neill too was furious. Arum saw him after the fight and said the House Speaker was "disgusted" by the decision. O'Neill ran into Bob Halloran, a Massachusetts native and former Miami sportscaster who was then president of Caesars Sports.

"You can tell the promoters," O'Neill warned Halloran, "that if Marvin doesn't get another title shot, there will be an investigation."

Marvin was not only frustrated at getting another awful decision, he was heartbroken for his fans, Goody and Pat, Bertha and his kids, and, most of all, Ida Mae.

"For all the people who wanted to see me win the title, I feel bad. But the one person I wanted to win the title for the most was my mom, my greatest fan," he said. "What am I going to have to do, kill somebody to get this for her and my family?"

Boston Globe sportswriter, Leigh Montville, who had covered Marvin for years, said Marvin fought to Antuofermo's level and it cost him.

"Marvin a lot of times respected people too much when he fought them the first time," Montville said. "I think he respected Vito too much and wound up in a draw. He probably won but it was close."

Bertha watched the post-fight interviews and made her way to the locker room to console her man. They hugged and she assured Marvin that his day would come. After he showered and changed, they walked hand-in-hand down the hall out of the arena and into Caesar's casino.

"No matter what the judges said, as far as I'm concerned I am the middleweight champion," he said. "I know I won that fight tonight."

Duane Ford, the judge who scored it in Hagler's favor, would forever proudly tell friends and media that he was the judge who got the Antuofermo–Hagler fight right.

Also in the crowd at Caesars that night was Alan Minter, the number-two contender in the world. While Antuofermo said post-fight that he would grant Marvin a rematch—and Arum agreed—the rematch did not happen. Instead, Alan's promoter Mickey Duff pressed Arum to give Minter a shot—as required by the rules. Minter was granted a shot and the title fight was set for Las Vegas between Alan and Antuofermo on March 16, 1980.

While it was yet another insult to Marvin, it was a shot at glory for Alan, plus a chance for him to bolster British boxing and bring the world title back to the UK.

TRAGEDY FOR MINTER

Like Marvin in the US, in Europe Alan Minter was a rising star, climbing the ranks in search of a title shot.

While Alan prepared to challenge the champion, cuts continued to haunt him. He worked with his trainers on his defense and footwork. He had the punching power and the skill but he could never be world champion if his eyebrows opened up gushing blood every time he got hit.

"He had to box a little cleverer, instead of going in all guns blazing," Mick Minter said. "He was boxing better. His timing became better."

He married his trainer Doug Bidwell's daughter Lorraine. They built a four-bedroom house just outside Crawley and started a family. His plastering days behind him, Alan was a celebrity in his hometown, and across England. He trained hard but still enjoyed a few pints at the pub.

He trained with former British featherweight champion Bobby Neill and became the British middleweight champ by narrowly defeating Kevin Finnegan in a fifteen-round war at Royal Albert Hall. It was the first of three legendary fights between Alan and Finnegan, all of which Alan won. To this day, they are some of the most memorable fights in British boxing history.

In 1977 in Milan, Alan won the European middleweight belt by knocking out Germano Valsecchi in the fifth round. A few months later in Monaco, Alan ended the career of Marvin's idol, Emile Griffith, winning a ten-round decision in Griffith's final bout.

Six weeks later, in September 1977, Alan lost his European title to hard-punching Italian middleweight Gratien Tonna. The fight was stopped in the eighth due to a massive gash across Alan's forehead and Tonna was awarded the TKO victory.

He reclaimed his British title two months later, in November 1977, once again defeating Finnegan in a fifteen-round decision at Wembley Arena. On July 19, 1978, Alan's life changed forever. That night, he stepped into the ring at Municipal Stadium in Bellaria, Italy, to battle Angelo Jacopucci, an Italian middleweight contender, who had a record of 33-2 with seven knockouts, for the vacant European middleweight title. The Italian crowd firmly backed the blonde-haired, chiseled Italian as he fought valiantly against the more powerful and brutish Brit. In the twelfth round, fatigue set in and Jacopucci, tragically, lowered his guard.

Alan pounced and pummeled the Italian's face, reminding spectators why he was nicknamed "Boom Boom." Jacopucci's head snapped back several times before he went limp and fell to the canvas. He was out cold and Alan was declared the winner by KO. The Italian crowd was quiet as their fighter lay motionless.

There was immediate concern that the fight should have been stopped sooner. After a few minutes, Jacopucci woke up. He was helped to his feet and raised his arms, assuring fans he was OK. He wasn't.

The twenty-nine-year-old boxer left the arena and went with friends to dinner, where he encountered Alan in the restaurant. The two fighters exchanged pleasantries. The Italian was still woozy, had a horrible headache, and vomited. He returned to his hotel where his symptoms worsened. His trainers called for an ambulance and he was brought to a hospital first in Rimini, and then to a trauma center in Bologna where he underwent emergency surgery to relieve bleeding on his brain. He went into a coma for two days.

On July 22, 1978, three days after the fight, Jacopucci was removed from life support and declared dead. The young fighter's death devastated Alan. It also led to criminal charges against the referee, Jacopucci's manager, and the ring doctor. The referee and manager were acquitted but the ring doctor was found guilty of manslaughter for not halting the beating.

The death was not the first time boxing was forced to look at its rules and take action to make the sport safer. In the wake of the tragedy, European title fights were reduced from fifteen rounds to twelve.

"It was sickening really," Mick Minter says. "You could see when Alan hit him, Jacopucci was bouncing off the ropes and . . . you could tell something wasn't right from the look on Jacopucci's face as he went down."

Winning the European title again and moving up the rankings should have been cause for celebration. But Jacopucci's death cast a pall over Alan.

"It was very somber really. The excitement had gone obviously because of the thought of what happened," Mick Minter remembers.

Jacopucci's wife was furious and spoke out in the press after he died. She blamed Alan for his death, which was difficult for him, according to his brother.

"He kept his thoughts and feelings to himself, but it did affect him," Mick Minter said. "He had good people around him. He soldiered on. . . . It wasn't his fault. Alan was just there to do a job and that's what it's all about."

Four months later, in November 1978, Alan was back in the ring at Wembley, defending his European title and getting revenge on Tonna, nicknamed "The Marseilles Mauler," whom Alan had lost to a year earlier. Tonna was mercurial and came into their rematch with forty-two wins and five losses. His biggest fight was in 1975 when he was knocked out in the fifth round while challenging iconic champion Carlos Monzon. Monzon, who retired in 1977 as the longest-reigning undisputed middleweight champion, led a tragic life after retiring from the sport. He was a monster outside of the ring who had a long record of abusing women and once famously claimed that he beat every woman in his life.

In 1973, while world champion, he was shot in the leg by his wife Mercedes Beatriz García. In 1974, he was accused of beating paparazzi. He was arrested or detained by authorities many times throughout his violent life for assaulting women.

He dated Swiss bombshell actress Ursula Andress. In 1979, he married Uruguayan model Alicia Muniz and had a son. But the relationship was volatile. In 1988, while staying in the Argentine seaside resort city Mar Del Plata, he beat and strangled Alicia before tossing her off a second-floor balcony, killing her.

He leaped after her and was injured but survived the fall and was charged with murder. Monzon got eleven years in prison for killing his wife. He died in a 1995 car accident while speeding back to jail returning from furlough.

While perhaps not quite as ruthlessly violent as Monzon, Tonna too had a dark side. He was disliked by the French boxing world and had a bad reputation as a thug. In 1976, he was charged with involuntary homicide and drunk driving when he sped through a work zone and slammed his vehicle into Marseilles police officer Jean Forassassi, killing the cop. He received a one-year jail sentence but served just six months.

A few weeks after he was released from prison, in March 1977, he was shot during a melee in a Marseilles pub, reportedly while protecting a prostitute.

Alan, on the other hand, liked a drink but mostly avoided trouble, outside of the occasional pub scuffle. He and Tonna met again on November 7, 1979, at Wembley Arena. Alan faced a slew of questions about Jacopucci. But what was there to say?

Alan felt awful, but was certain he could have done nothing differently. He disliked that he had killed a man in the ring. But he did nothing illegal, or outside the rules, so he accepted the Italian fighter's death and tried to move on, even if the press would not let him.

"How does a man overcome the knowledge that a fellow fighter died from brain injuries suffered at his hands?" Newcastle *Evening Chronicle* boxing writer John Marquis wrote. "How can he ever recapture the ruthlessness and venom?"

Marquis profiled Alan as he sparred at Thomas à Becket Pub in London's Old Kent Road.

"I am a professional," Alan told him. "It is my job to fight and I am nothing without boxing. I have to keep going."

But in an exclusive first-person piece in the *Sunday Mirror* a few days before the fight, Alan admitted vulnerability. His wife Lorraine was about to give birth to their second child and he struggled to put the death of Jacopucci and his future into perspective.

"There were, of course, moments when I thought I would not fight again," Alan wrote. "There were nights of sleepless misery . . . Will the misery which haunted me after the death of that gallant Italian come flooding back?"

He told the paper that he overcame the tragedy largely through the hundreds of letters he received "from strangers all over the world offering sympathy and help."

Minter also recalled being in a pub after the fatal fight and overheard a man say to a friend: "I supposed we will have to call him 'Killer Minter' now."

Alan worked hard to steer the press away from the Jacopucci darkness and focused on Tonna.

"He's a typical bully boy," Alan said. "When he's hitting you and hurting you he loves it . . . but when you start rattling back at him he tends to go a bit. When he's got to take some, he doesn't love the game quite so much."

He added: "I don't like Tonna. When I know it's time for the knockout drop, I'll place my shot to have the most devastating effect . . . even if some unthinkable fan is yelling, 'Kill him Alan!'"

He went a step further, telling reporters the night before the fight that the Jacopucci tragedy drove him to win the world title once and for all. In his mind, he believed he owed it to the fallen Italian fighter.

"All that has happened has simply made me more determined than ever to be world champion," he said. "I want to show that Jacopucci, who put up a heroic fight, was beaten by a future world champion. Not some bum."

It was true boxer's logic. Alan was in the best shape of his career and, despite the tragedy, was in the best frame of mind of his life. Tonna paid the price.

Alan was faster, stronger, and smarter and landed shot after shot. In the third round, Tonna looked to the referee after Alan rocked him with a right at the bell. Tonna headbutted Alan at one point, but it did not shake him and he took it to Tonna through five rounds. As the bell rang to start the sixth, Tonna raised his hand in defeat and quit, giving Alan the victory.

"Minter had forecast that Tonna would quit once things started to go against him," Colin Hart, a writer for *The Sun* wrote. "And he couldn't have been more right."

The victory was a relief for Alan, who won his next four fights and became the number-one contender.

Doug Bidwell was sure that his fighter was on his way to a world title.

"When you think of all the problems Alan has had in his career and the way he has risen above them, you know he is something special," Bidwell said.

WORLD CHAMPION ALAN MINTER

Back in Brockton, Marvin continued thumping the heavy bag, doing his roadwork, and sending sparring partners to the showers at Petronelli Brothers Gym. He was sick to his stomach about being denied a rematch against Vito Antuofermo.

"Just keep winning, Stuff," Pat Petronelli told him. "You'll get your shot again."

Marvin stayed the course. In February 1980, he was matched up with Algerian Olympian Loucif Hamani in Portland, Maine. Marvin was not happy to be fighting in Maine again after his Vegas experience, but he listened to his team.

Antuofermo was ringside as Marvin stepped in to face Hamani. Arum was watching. His goal was to time Marvin's matches right so he could maximize his star power in a big title fight during TV sweeps.

"Marvin Hagler is more marketable than ever," Arum said.

"Rather than go right into an immediate rematch," Arum said, "The strategy, if both fighters continue to win, is to wait until September because September is the new ratings season, the time when you can get the most money."

Marvin was lined up for a $70,000 nationally-televised payday for the Hamani fight. Still, Marvin was wary of the sport's judges and politics.

"These are going to do my talking," he said, raising his fists in the prefight press conference.

Hamani, who was 20-1 coming into the fight, lost to Alan Minter in the 1972 Olympics. At the Portland arena, four thousand fans braved a blizzard to watch a short fight in which the European fighter paid a price.

Marvin knocked him around the ring in the first round before he hit Hamani with a hard shot that drove him through the ropes just forty seconds into the second round. He landed at Goody's feet, the trainer catching Hamani's head in his hands before it smashed upon the hard wooden floor. Goody tended to Hamani and gave him smelling salts while Marvin's hands were raised in victory by the referee.

"He was out cold," Goody said of the Algerian. "He was out for five minutes."

Marvin told the press afterwards that he had Antuofermo on his mind as he attacked Hamani.

"Once I saw he was hurt I got vicious," Marvin said. "I let Vito slide . . . when I should have had him."

Antuofermo watched the fight and left the arena quietly after the KO.

Marvin was resolute, saying: "I'm looking like a champion and I want another shot at the title. All I want is another shot at Vito."

A month later, Marvin and the Petronellis flew to Vegas to watch Alan fight Antuofermo at Caesars.

Marvin, Goody, Pat, Wainwright, and the rest of the entourage made their way through Caesars' casino the night before the fight. They ran into Alan and his camp. The Brit put his hand out to greet Marvin. Goody and Pat flanked their young fighter. Marvin ignored the handshake, glared at Alan, and stalked off.

Antuofermo did a lot of talking before the fight. He was being heavily marketed at the time as a middleweight version of Sylvester Stallone's *Rocky*. He emigrated to Brooklyn from Italy when he was just fifteen.

"When I came to the United States I could speak no English," Antuofermo said. "I had to find work but that was not possible for me for a long time in New York."

His life changed during a street fight when a cop broke it up. The officer was Italian and spoke to young Vito in his native language, telling him: "If you want to fight, why don't you go to a gym and learn to box."

He pointed him to the Police Athletic League gym in Brooklyn, where Antuofermo trained as an amateur.

"I never forgot that man," Antuofermo said. "I would like to say thank you because that cop certainly changed my life."

Antuofermo talked about the fight against Marvin and said: "He did not do nearly enough to take my title from me."

Despite receiving nine stitches to close a cut to his brow during the fight, Antuofermo brashly predicted he would dominate if they met again.

"I took the heart out of him," Antuofermo said. "He won't be the same guy if I ever fight him again."

Alan too took shots at Marvin in the prefight press conference. Speaking of how he would beat Antuofermo when Marvin could not, Alan said: "Hagler ran out of steam after eight rounds. I won't."

On fight night, Alan was in top form. He went out and fought hard against Antuofermo in a battle of two notorious bleeders.

"You can breathe on these guys and draw blood," Howard Cosell said.

Marvin sat ringside with Goody and Pat, stoic. He watched in disgust.

Alan and Antuofermo went the distance, both bleeding slightly from cuts above the eyes by the twelfth round, but neither suffered any of the bad cuts for which they had become known. Alan was knocked down in the fourteenth, but he claimed after the fight it was a slip after Antuofermo shoved him.

"Alan has never been off his feet," his manager/father-in-law Doug Bidwell said. "So why should he go down from a shove to the chest? He slipped."

When the final bell sounded, both fighters thought they had won. It was a split decision. American judge Charles Minker scored it 144-141 for Alan. Venezuelan judge Ladaslad Sanchez had 145-143 for Antuofermo.

The British judge, Roland Dakin, scored it a lopsided 149-137 for his countryman, handing Alan the middleweight title. Alan erupted in jubilation as the decision was announced. He was the first British challenger to win a title in America since Ted "Kid" Lewis in Boston in 1912. The New York *Daily News* called it a "hometown decision—8,000 miles from home."

Alan ignored the analysts. In his post-fight interview, he told the thousand-plus raucous Englishmen in the crowd that drinks were on him at Caesars.

"I made history," he declared.

He was twenty-seven years old, married, had a sixteen-month-old son, Ross, at home and another baby on the way and now was about to return to the pubs of England as a world champion. Back in Crawley, England, Alan's supporters emptied from the pubs and overran the streets as the victory was announced. He returned home—three stitches above his eye and hobbling from a strained ankle ligament caused by a knockdown in the fight—to a massive parade in his honor.

There were immediate post-fight reports that Marvin would get the first shot at Alan's title, but instead it was Antuofermo who was given a rematch.

Arum and British fight promoter Harry Levene announced the rematch after reports surfaced that the British judge, Roland Dakin, was corrupt. Dakin, it turned out, had flown on the plane from London to Las Vegas with Alan and his entourage. Not only that, Arum says Dakin gave a "thumbs up" to the BBC broadcaster after every round, signaling that Alan won.

Antuofermo was incensed.

"I'm an Italian citizen. Why wasn't there an Italian judge?" Antuofermo said.

"The system is wrong," Arum said. "You bring in an English judge who scores the fight so one-sided that Vito was going into this fight with two impartial officials and one man who came in as partisan for his country. It's a lousy, rotten system."

A month later, on April 20, 1980, Marvin returned again to Portland, Maine—instead of Vegas—to fight. This time, he had his shot at revenge against the one Philadelphia fighter he had never beaten: Boogaloo Watts. It had been more than four years since Marvin went into The Spectrum as an undefeated up-and-comer and was robbed.

"This is the one that counts," Marvin said in his prefight press conference. "I was a different fighter four years ago."

Marvin was paid $100,000 for the nationally-televised fight and left nothing to the judges. After a first round in which the two fighters traded sharp jabs, Watts came looking for a fight in the second—and got it. He threw a wild right that missed Marvin and Watts spun around and fell to the canvas. When he got up, Marvin pounced, rocking his head with an uppercut followed by a combination that knocked Watts back to the canvas.

A few seconds later, Marvin snapped a hard straight right into Watts's unprotected face that knocked him down again. He tried to rise to his feet as the round came to an end but collapsed and was counted out, giving Marvin the KO victory. Marvin dedicated the victory to his former sparring partner and friend, Andrea McCoy, a New Bedford middleweight who was one of twenty-two members of the US Olympic boxing team killed in a plane that crashed en route to Poland for an exhibition.

"What I wanted to do was set this man up and put his lights out solidly," Marvin said in his post-fight interview on ABC. "I figured that they would take it from me . . . so I couldn't make it that way, so I had to hurt him. When I knew he was hurt, I stayed on him."

A month later, Bob Arum brought Marvin back to Caesars to face Marcos Geraldo, a Mexican contender who was 53-15 and had lost a close battle to Sugar Ray Leonard a few months earlier. The fight took place on May 17, 1980, and went the distance. Marvin won a unanimous decision, which cemented his status as the number-one contender.

Alan and Antuofermo were preparing for their rematch at London's Wembley Arena, but Marvin was busy taking care of something far more important outside the ring. In June 1980, he and Bertha got married.

"Who is your best friend?" Marvin was asked by renowned boxing columnist Red Smith.

"Bertha," he answered.

He and Bertha were planning to build a new house and Marvin, while still seeking another title shot, for the first time talked publicly about his future beyond boxing. He said he might put his masonry skills to use, which he learned in his early days with Goody and Pat's construction company.

He looked and sounded like a more mature fighter and man. Gone was the early-career poetry and bravado. By 1980, Marvin had fought for a world title and had seen the ugly side of the sport up close. He was finally making real money and was now a family man, something he made official when he married Bertha. The press, too, was starting to take interest in Marvin.

The *Boston Globe* ran a front-page feature on Bertha calling her "Mrs. Marvelous." In interviews, he said he loved playing backgammon, gin rummy, and ping-pong with his friends and family, as well as the popular new video games Pac-Man and Space Invaders, which had just hit the market. He talked about his love of music. His favorite singer was Lena Horne. He also loved the TV shows *Barnaby Jones* and *M.A.S.H.* His favorite athlete: Julius Erving.

Life was good for Marvin. The hellscape he grew up in in Newark was far behind him and now he had money, nice clothes, cars, a family, and fame. But he still wanted the title.

The press had taken to calling him "the uncrowned middleweight champion."

THE NATIONAL FRONT

After beating Boogaloo Watts and Marcos Geraldo, Marvin could only wait. Goody, Pat, and Steve Wainright had called in every favor. Bob Arum knew it was Marvin's time. He promised him another title shot against the winner of the Minter–Antuofermo rematch. Marvin appealed to reporters every chance he got. His frustration consumed him.

"Minter is only champion because he gained the benefit of the beating I gave to Antuofermo in Las Vegas," Marvin said.

Marvin did not go to the fight at Wembley, choosing instead to stay home with his new wife and kids. He took out his anger on sparring partners at Petronelli Brothers Gym as he and Goody worked to prepare for the winner of the title fight.

Antuofermo arrived in London to jeers from Alan's supporters, which now included members of the National Front, a white nationalist group that still exists today as a far-right conservative political party in England.

Founded in 1967, but with roots stretching back to the global fascism movement of the 1930s, the National Front is a neo-Nazi organization that promotes racial-separatist propaganda. Only whites can join. The group has consistently pushed white-replacement conspiracy theories, practiced anti-Semitism, and denied the Holocaust.

In the eighties, the group attracted football hooligans and neo-Nazi skinheads, many of whom looked to Alan as an inspiration for the white power movement. He had, after all, won the middleweight title in the US after beating several Black fighters. By becoming the first British world champion in years, Alan invigorated the National Front.

The group, which uses the Union Jack as its logo, protested British immigration policies and pushed for laws banning marriages between Brits and "non-Aryans." In 1980, the NF conducted an anti-immigration propaganda campaign that included plastering posters across London depicting menacing pictures of dreadlocked Blacks to stoke fear among whites. The posters declared that the National Front was the white race's "Last Chance" to save Britain.

NF members were known to go out and randomly chase down and beat immigrants and Blacks, and spraypaint racial slurs and NF slogans all over South London. They held rallies calling for immigrants to be kicked out of Britain.

The group also had a history of political violence. In 1974, a student protester was killed by a police officer during a clash between the NF and leftists in Red Lion Square in Central London.

In 1976, eighteen-year-old Sikh student Gurdip Singh Chaggar was attacked by hooligans in South London who beat and stabbed him to death. After the killing, NF chairman John Kingsley said: "One down, one million to go."

In 1977, the NF was at the center of widespread rioting that occurred during the "Battle of Lewisham," which pitted the white supremacists against Blacks, socialists, and anarchists. The clashes were marked by firebombings and beatings as the NF targeted leftist newspapers in London. In April 1979, New-Zealand-born teacher and activist Blair Peach was killed during anti-racist demonstrations in Southall, London, when the NF clashed with protesters. Peach was killed from a blow to the head from a Metropolitan Police Service officer.

The violence continued as the decade ended, escalating when an entire Asian family was murdered in a house fire sparked by a petroleum bomb lobbed into the house. No one was ever charged with the crime that killed a mother and her three children, but police believed the bombing was the work of the NF, which had been regularly attacking Asians in the area.

The racial unrest that permeated the country was palpable when Antuofermo and Alan met at Wembley. Alan never publicly claimed to be a member of the NF but he never distanced himself from the group either. In fact, he had spoken at their rallies and embraced their ranks as he did all his fans.

The fight was promoted by Alan's longtime promoter Mickey Duff, a legendary boxing figure who escaped Nazi Germany as a child and started boxing at age fifteen, lying about his age so he could fight for money. The son of a rabbi, Duff was born in Poland and fled the Nazi invasion with his family in 1937, landing in London where they slept in tube stations during the London Blitz.

Duff quit fighting after seventy bouts, losing only eight, and became a matchmaker and fight promoter. He went on to become one of the most influential people in British boxing. He joined forces with manager Harry Levene and together they promoted Muhammad Ali's bout against British hero Henry Cooper at Arsenal's Highbury Stadium in North London before forty thousand fans. At the time, it was the biggest spectacle the sport had seen in the United Kingdom. Now, he and Levene were cashing in on Alan's newfound celebrity.

After winning the title, Alan, with his blue eyes and chiseled features, was given six-figure endorsement deals from fashion brands. Posters of him dotted the London subway stations that showed him dressed sharply in sports clothes with the slogan "The Cool Taste of Mint."

Duff capitalized on the fanfare, knowing he had a star on his hands. A legendary gambler, Duff once lost $225,000 on the tables in a single night in the '70s—a huge sum by today's standards. He was also a paid fight consultant for Caesars. Like most in the fight game in the sixties, seventies, and eighties, organized crime loomed around him constantly. After Duff barred the Kray Twins from a fight he promoted for Sugar Ray Robinson, the ruthless London mobsters sent Duff's wife a gift-wrapped box that contained four dead rats.

He was constantly at odds with fellow UK promoter Frank Warren as they fought for the rights to many of the major British fighters of the era, much like King and Arum in the United States. When Warren was shot point-blank in the chest in 1989 on a London street, Duff was asked by the press about who might have wanted to shoot Warren.

"It couldn't have been anyone in boxing. They wouldn't have missed," Duff said.

World champion fighter Terry Marsh was charged in the shooting but was acquitted at trial and no one else was ever charged. For Duff, the title fight between Alan and Antuofermo was another huge coup for him and his legacy.

Alan, too, knew the stakes of the fight. He was the first Brit to defend his title in his homeland in years. He trained hard and told the press before the fight that he was "As sharp as I've ever been."

Antuofermo was equally confident: "I have come here to get my title back and I will be leaving with it."

But it was Alan's night. Their second match didn't resemble the close fight that Alan won controversially in Vegas a few months earlier. This time Alan outboxed Antuofermo and busted him up badly. The fight ended as blood streamed down the Italian fighter's face and he refused to get off his stool to start the ninth round. Alan was awarded the TKO victory, giving him his first successful title defense and sending the sold-out crowd into a frenzy.

The next day the *Sunday Mirror* of London featured the headline: "BLOODBATH" (with a picture of Antuofermo's battered face). The *Sunday Sun* of London headline read: "MINTER MAGIC."

"Alan Minter gave the show of his career," *The Sun* wrote.

The next day, Arum announced that Marvin would get a shot at Alan's title in England.

"If Minter wants the Hagler fight, it can be delivered immediately," Arum said.

Marvin watched the fight at a resort in Hawaii with Bertha on their honeymoon. It was a nice vacation but, as soon as the fight was over, Marvin started planning his training schedule to get ready to go get the belt.

"We'll put the show on at Buckingham Palace if necessary," Steve Wainwright told the press.

WAR OF WORDS IN LONDON

Marvin flew back to Logan Airport and went right into training. Goody and Pat were already lining up sparring partners, one of whom was Marvin's younger brother, Robbie Sims, who had just turned pro as a middleweight a few months earlier.

Sims, aka "Rockin' Robbie," had two pro fights when he and Marvin squared off in an exhibition at Massasoit Community College in Brockton. Marvin, Goody, and Pat headed to Provincetown where Marvin again locked himself in "prison." This time, he would not leave anything go the judges. He knew he was going into Alan's backyard and had to not only fight well, but knock the Brit out.

"Destruction and destroy," Marvin said. "That's my only talk. Destruction and destroy."

In *The Sun* newsroom on London's Fleet Street, a sports editor approached the paper's boxing writer Colin Hart, holding up a picture of Marvin. Hart had covered Alan's career for years and was one of the foremost authorities on the fight game in Britain at the time.

"Who is this guy?" the editor asked. "Well why don't you go over to the States and interview him before he comes to Britain for the Minter fight?"

Hart got a phone number for Goody, called the trainer, and made arrangements to visit them in Provincetown. Hart hopped on a plane to Logan and got a car for the two-and-a-half-hour ride to Provincetown.

"I'd never heard of Provincetown before," Hart recalled. "I didn't realize it was the gay capital of the Eastern Seaboard. I thought, *Does this mean Marvin is gay?*"

Of course, Hart knew Marvin was just back from his honeymoon and Hart knew he was straight, but he did find it an odd choice for training camp, as many did. That is until they visited and saw the desolation of the town in the off-season. The town is different today thanks to WiFi and remote work but back in 1980 it was as seasonal a community as existed in the United States. While summertime saw the town overrun with tourists and a population that swelled to sixty-thousand-plus, there were just two to three thousand year-round residents, making it feel almost like a ghost town at times. Walking down Commercial Street in August was very different than September, when the quiet would often only be interrupted by the sound of waves crashing on the beach or the occasional passing car or bicycle. It was just how Marvin liked it. No distractions.

The prefight hype was well underway when Hart landed in P-town and it featured the usual bravado with each fighter bragging and predicting victory. But things suddenly got ugly when Alan said something that ended up making global headlines.

The BBC quoted Alan as saying about Marvin: "No Black man is going to take my title." Another report was that Alan said: "I have no intention of losing my title to a Black man."

Either version immediately ratcheted up the stakes of the fight. It was just the fuel that the National Front needed as they ramped up their domestic campaign of terror.

Hart had just heard about the remark when he arrived in Provincetown and was led to one of the town's only open dive bars on Commercial Street. A stranger in a strange land, he felt like he was in an old James

Cagney movie when he pushed open the heavy, wooden door and saw two figures in tracksuits sitting across the smoky barroom. It was Goody and Pat.

Hart walked over and extended a hand to them both. Goody shook his hand firmly and pulled Hart in close.

"Hey look, I'm sorry Colin, but Marvin has refused to speak with you," Goody told him.

Hart was flabbergasted.

"I've come three thousand miles at tremendous expense," he said. "Is there something we can do here? I need to get my story."

Goody looked at Pat, who shook his head.

"Look Colin," Goody said. "Marvin is now convinced that anyone from Britain is a racist."

It was emotional blackmail, Hart thought to himself. He wrung his hands.

"Look mate, I'm going to lose my job over this," Hart told him, begging. "I've got two kids."

Goody took pity on the young writer.

"Calm down," he told him. "I don't want you losing your job. Let me talk to him."

Looking back, Hart laughed, saying: "It was a bit of bullshit because I wouldn't have lost my job."

But it worked. Goody went to Marvin and explained that the young guy out in the bar had traveled from England just to tell the people back in London the real story of the man fighting their hero—the story of Marvelous Marvin Hagler.

"Marvin relented and agreed to meet me," Hart says.

They spent several hours together. Marvin bared his soul.

"There's a monster that comes out of me in the ring," he said. "I think it goes back to the days when I had nothing. It's hunger, I think. That's what the monster is and it's still there."

Hart got his story and England got a full picture of the man about to enter Wembley Arena to fight their hero.

The racial dimension of the match only grew. Some said Marvin hated white people. He certainly didn't trust authority, especially the white establishment.

The narrative of the fight spun over and over. Minter was the working-class hero who twice beat the man Marvin could not—Vito Antuofermo. Marvin was the angry ghetto kid who escaped Newark and had a chip on his shoulder.

From the moment Marvin got off the plane at Heathrow Airport on September 17, 1980, wearing his trademark dark shades, "WAR" trucker cap, and a white buttoned-down shirt, he felt the tension. He carried his own bags as he walked out of the airport, ignoring assembled media, and got into a car for his camp, which would occupy a space upstairs from a pub in Lavender Hill, Battersea.

When Marvin stepped into the smoky pub in London, he carried the weight of his past. He was a product of the Newark riots and the desperation of Brockton's industrial blight.

Marvin was as focused as he had ever been and sparred heavily with journeyman Danny Snyder, a southpaw, and his brother Robbie. He beat up both—especially his brother. Goody and Pat had to tell Marvin more than once to take it easy on his sparring partners.

Bertha made the trip across the Atlantic with Robbie, Ida Mae, and Steven Wainwright. They played tourist for the first couple days, visiting Picadilly

Circus, where they saw punk rockers with safety pins, purple and orange hair, and denim and leather jackets. They went to Buckingham Palace and watched the changing of the guards.

Marvin's entourage was put up at Bailey's Hotel and Alan's promoter, Mickey Duff, got them a van with a driver, a twenty-one-year-old former boxer who stopped at a lot of pay phones. At first Marvin and Goody thought he might be a bookie, but they soon figured out he was a spy for Duff and Alan.

Boxing writers Leigh Montville, of the *Boston Globe*, and the *Boston Herald*'s George Kimball, along with Frank Stoddard of Marvin's hometown paper, the *Brockton Enterprise*, covered the event while the broader boxing press was back in Vegas to covering the Larry Holmes–Muhammad Ali fight. Kimball, Montville, Wainwright, and others convened daily for drinks at the Stanhope Arms, a pub across the street from their hotel.

"Kimball got us all going to the bar at twelve-noon until two in the afternoon," Montville recalled. "Then at two in the afternoon, it was last call, so you got, like, seven beers. You'd go back to your room, drink, and then take a nap and then go back because Marvin trained at night. And then we filed our stories."

While the boozy trio of Boston sportswriters, led by Wainwright, followed Marvin around London, Marvin was tight-lipped. He didn't want to talk politics.

The bad blood between Marvin and Alan intensified a few days before the fight when the British media reported that Marvin refused to shake Kevin Finnegan's hand before they fought in Vegas the previous year. According to the report—one seemingly concocted in a Fleet Street newsroom to increase racial animus and deflect from Alan's racist comment—Marvin said he would not shake Finnegan's hand because: "I don't touch white flesh."

Marvin denied the accusation, telling the press: "I make a point of never shaking hands with future opponents." He did, in fact, shake hands with Finnegan post-fight, he said, as he did with all his opponents.

Nevertheless, the headline went global. But it did not take long for responsible reporters to clarify the record, including Colin Malam, a boxing writer at London's *Daily Telegraph*.

Malam interviewed Finnegan who denied Marvin made a comment about "white flesh," and recalled what he heard the Brockton fighter say: "I never touch flesh before we get into the ring."

Finnegan said it was a sarcastic exchange and that he played along, telling Marvin: "And what makes you think you'll touch mine once we're in there."

The clarifications aside, much of the media continued to run with the narrative that Marvin also made a racist comment, which signaled to Alan's National Front base that Marvin was an angry Black man who hated whites.

Marvin shrugged off the controversy.

"He will pay for saying that when we meet at Wembley," he told reporters.

THE FIGHT

Dogged about the "Black man" comment, Alan tried in vain to explain it. He told the press that he said he would not lose his title to "that Black man," as if that were better. It was, to be fair, 1980, a time when racial sensitivities were not what they are today in Britain or the US.

"Minter had a lot of support among extreme right-wing racists," Colin Hart said. "They were members of the National Front and they were definitely racists, anti-black, and antisemitic. There were quite a lot of National Front people who supported Minter."

Alan's brother, Mick Minter, who was with him throughout the fight and in the days before, said his brother never denied making the comment, but felt bad about it.

"He stood by what he said," Mick Minter said. "The racial side of it stayed with him for quite a long time."

While the tension simmered, the prefight weigh-in caused its own controversy. Marvin showed up to a throng of press in the ring in Wembley, stripped down to his underwear, and stepped on the scale. He was overweight by a half-pound.

Marvin, Goody, and Pat argued with the officials about the scale, saying Marvin weighed in at an even 160 pounds that morning. So the officials suggested Marvin get on the scale naked. Two ring-card girls working for liquor sponsors were asked to leave the ring. They left and Marvin came out in his jock strap. He was still three ounces over.

The officials gave him two hours to lose the three ounces, while Alan walked to the scale. Alan looked trim and fit. He wore a blue scally cap and stripped down to his Union Jack briefs. He had an army of fans cheering him as he stepped on the scale and was four ounces under the limit.

A half-hour later Marvin returned, again stripped down to his jock strap, and stepped on the scale—exactly 160 pounds.

"I weighed myself in this morning and was one-sixty," Marvin told a BBC announcer. "I was surprised about the scale here. But I've been through this before. I'm just going to take it out on Minter now."

Asked how he dropped the weight, he replied: "That's my secret. That's a fighter's secret. You don't want to reveal that."

With Alan just a few feet away, Marvin revealed his plan.

"All I want to do is destroy and destruct this man and take this championship that I think is mine," Marvin said.

Alan was relaxed and nonchalant, joking about his Union Jack underwear and keeping it light.

"I feel nice and well," Alan told the announcer. "I'll be glad when it's all over."

His brother Mick said Alan had been partying heavily in the pubs since winning the title and perhaps did not train as hard as he should have—especially for a fight against a boxer of Marvin's caliber.

"He might have taken him a bit lightly," Mick Minter said.

On fight night, Marvin, wearing trunks and a hooded robe made of maroon velour, stalked toward the ring flanked by Goody and Pat. The brothers wore dark blue work shirts and jeans and looked like auto mechanics. Boos rained down on Marvin as he made his way through the alcohol-fueled British crowd, whose jeers muffled "The Star-Spangled Banner." Marvin stared straight ahead, his eyes focused on the ring.

It was clear to many there that night that something was off.

"The night of the fight, I go to Wembley and I notice before the fight there's all these skinhead guys," Leigh Montville said. "Minter was a very British nationalist guy. All these skinhead guys were fans of his with the shaved heads and the Doc Martin boots. They're buying cases of beer. I had never seen cases of beers sold at a fight. They'd buy a case of beer, put it on their shoulder and go up to the third deck."

The cases contained glass bottles. Wembley was a powderkeg.

Arum had attended countless title fights but that night was different. He had a bad feeling.

"The arena as I remember was filled with white supremacists, white nationalists," he said. "It was really not a great atmosphere."

Bertha was scared. She heard the taunts, saw the drunkenness, felt the danger. She had an American flag she planned to wave, but kept it folded under her seat.

"When they [the fighters] started getting into the ring, it was scary, because you had a lot of angry English over there. And we were Black," she said.

Alan, a few inches taller than Marvin, wore Union Jack trunks and walked into the ring behind a Union Jack flag and a St. George's cross—a National Front symbol—while "God Save the Queen" blared.

"Minter, we discovered, and his father, were white nationalists—fascist bastards," Arum said later.

In the arena hooligans ripped up pro-Hagler banners, tearing them from American fans' hands. As Marvin was introduced, the crowd booed him, and the boos grew louder when "The Star-Spangled Banner" played. Several hooligans dropped their pants and mooned the ring during the anthem.

BBC commentator Harry Carpenter described the scene: "Wembley Arena was reeking, not so much of nationalism, but had a decidedly rancid smell of racialism." He later criticized the venue for not limiting alcohol sales.

The boxers faced each other in the center of the ring, listening to the final instructions from referee Carlos Berrocal. Taller by an inch or two, Minter glared down at Hagler, who responded with an all-business stare. They did not shake hands. After Berrocal finished his instructions, the fighters glared at each other for a second more and turned back toward their corners.

Alan, in red trunks with white trim, loosened up in his corner and seemed full of nervous energy. He eyed Marvin across the ring. Marvin took some water from a bottle offered by Pat and bounced on his toes. As the bell rang, Goody gave his fighter's neck a squeeze and a small nudge that sent him off to battle.

Marvin and Alan met at center ring, where they circled each other and traded jabs for the first ten seconds. Then Minter opened up, throwing a combination that Hagler eluded by deftly rolling and leaning. The hooligans went wild when Minter went on the offensive. Hagler regained control of the distance before scoring with a sharp right. Although Minter was the aggressor early, Hagler counterpunched deftly.

When Minter closed the gap and tried mauling on the inside, Hagler connected with clubbing lefts and a right to the body. On defense, Hagler bobbed, weaved, and feinted, often making Minter miss and leaving him open to counters. With barely a minute gone, Minter was nicked under his right eye and beginning to bruise. A pair of jabs rocked Minter and an ensuing exchange saw Hagler get the best of it, closing with a roundhouse right that staggered Minter.

For the next forty-five seconds or so, the two middleweights jabbed, with Hagler slipping most of the incoming shots while pushing Minter back with hard rights from his southpaw stance. In response, Minter foolishly traded with his stronger, faster opponent. Minter landed a few isolated shots, but most of them were easily deflected by Marvin, whose defense was nearly impenetrable. Meanwhile, Marvin continued to land punishing blows, jarring Minter with a right twenty seconds before the bell. At the end of round one, Minter landed a blistering wind-up left to the jaw. But when the bell rang, Hagler walked confidently back to his corner. He was in charge.

As the second round began, Minter tried to box from the outside, hoping to minimize exchanges and land a power shot. For the first thirty seconds, Minter jabbed and circled to his right, while Hagler waited for an opening. Hagler made himself a hard target, and Minter struggled to connect. Hagler landed a snapping left counter over a jab and, a few seconds later, another left that made Minter clinch.

A minute into the second round, the two men threw straight lefts, landing simultaneously. Hagler stumbled after the exchange and an excited Minter waved his glove at him, defiantly, exhorting him to mix it up. Minter moved in to swap punches and Hagler calmly countered him with two right hooks, one of which left Minter bleeding from the nose. The fans chanted "Minter, Minter!" but it only seemed to prompt Marvin to accelerate. As Minter continued his ragged attack, Hagler picked his shots, landing hard lefts and rights, forcing Minter to clinch.

"Hagler [is] looking very, very good. Very sharp," Cosell commented.

A few seconds later, Minter scored with a left that seemed to stun Hagler. With Hagler retreating into the corner, Minter struck, throwing a series of lefts and rights; although the crowd erupted at the onslaught, Hagler eluded most of the blows before initiating a clinch. In the final seconds of the round, Minter again went on the attack. Hagler rushed forward and landed a stinging right uppercut and a sweeping left hand that sent Minter staggering at the bell.

Marvin returned to his corner, where Goody met him. "Nice work Marvin. Nice work," he said.

As the bell rang for the third, Goody, with a towel slung over his shoulder, leaned over the ropes and patted Marvin on his back.

"End this, Marvin. Let's go home," Goody said.

As they both came out for the third round, Marvin suddenly leaped forward with both feet and landed a devastating straight right to Alan's cheek that opened up another bloody wound.

"Wow!" Cosell said. "Hagler is fighting his fight."

Minter was bleeding from his nose, a cut under each eye, and a laceration above his left brow. As they exchanged blows, Alan stumbled backward. Marvin pounced when he saw an opening, scoring with two leaping right hooks that staggered Minter. Now bleeding profusely from the laceration above his left eye, Minter tried clinching to survive. But Hagler punished him with withering uppercuts on the inside. After they separated, they went toe-to-toe. A right hook and a straight left stunned Minter and another right shot his mouthpiece into the air. In hot pursuit, Hagler landed a sweeping right that sent Minter reeling into the corner.

"Minter's hurt! He's ready to go!" Cosell shouted. "Hagler is all over him!"

In clear pain, Minter grabbed his right eye as Hagler closed in, sensing the kill. With Minter in the corner, Hagler wound up another right hook that crashed into Minter's bloodied face. It might have been enough to end the fight. Instead, Hagler pounded Minter across the ring and into the ropes when referee Carlos Berrocal stepped between the two fighters. Berrocal frantically called for manager Doug Bidwell to inspect Minter.

Bidwell climbed the ring steps and examined Minter, whose brow looked like roadkill. He told Berrocal to stop the fight.

Marvin heard the exchange and saw Berrocal wave his arms, then stepped back and dropped to his knees in the center of the ring and raised his hands in victory. The belt—and respect—was his.

"A NATIONAL DISGRACE"

As Marvin, Goody, Pat, and Robbie Sims hugged in celebration in the center of the Wembley ring, a riot crashed around them.

"It was only the third round," Leigh Montville said. "All these skinhead guys, they still had eighteen beers left and they just started throwing them. The shit was just coming out of the sky. Fights were breaking out all around the arena."

Marvin, Goody, and Pat felt hard objects smash into their backs and heads. Minter's fans fired beer bottles and cans toward the ring, shouting epithets and threats.

Debris hit the ring as Robbie and the Petronelli brothers encircled Marvin, shielding him from the projectiles flying toward them. They protected Marvin while covering their own heads in terror as panic and bedlam took over the packed arena. People sitting ringside flipped their chairs over and held them over their heads to shield themselves from the bombardment from the upper level. A beer bottle hurled from the rafters smashed onto Pat Petronelli, spraying glass and beer all over him.

Bob Arum, Howard Cosell, and Rip Valenti dove for cover under the ring together. British police officers—the bobbies—stormed the ring, surrounded Marvin, and hustled him and the Petronelli brothers out of the arena under their cover. Marvin's family and entourage followed, ducking for cover as they fled for safety.

One rioter looked Bertha in the eye and sneered: "I hope your husband gets cancer." Bertha ran on in shock, tugging Ida Mae behind her. Ida Mae heard it too. She had lived through Newark but this was different.

"You could just see the look on her face," Bertha remembers of Ida Mae. "We had never been in a place before where they hated him. But he was Black and he whupped London's champion over there."

The terrified women were whisked out of the riot by cops and Marvin's entourage as bottles and debris continued to rain down.

Montville, *Boston Herald* writer George Kimball, and *Brockton Enterprise* writer Frank Stoddard shielded their heads with their typewriters. Normally, the writers would watch the fight until the end and bang out their stories on typewriters ringside before sending them back to their news desks. But that night, the typewriters were shields. They were under attack.

Vito Antuofermo sat next to them. He had been hired by Italian TV to provide color commentary for the fight. He grabbed Montville's arm.

"Follow me," he said.

As Antuofermo led the journalists toward the exit, a rioter smashed a beer bottle over the back of the fighter's head, apparently unaware of who he was.

"Vito turned around and whacked him. Right in the mouth," Montville said. "The guy went down like a sack of shit."

In his book *Four Kings*, Kimball said the right cross to the hooligan's face "may have been the best punch Antuofermo ever threw."

A bottle sailed through the air and struck BBC announcer Harry Carpenter on the head.

"There is chaos here, absolute chaos. I'm smothered in beer and so are all my colleagues around me," Carpenter said. He called the scene "a shame and a disgrace to British boxing."

John Merian Sr., a close friend of Marvin's from Brockton, fled his ringside seat and ran toward the tunnel with the rest of the entourage.

"My father was fearing for his life," his son, John Merian Jr., said. "They didn't know what to expect. This was a mob."

Later, Merian Sr. told his son: "I didn't know if we were going to get out of there alive."

As Marvin and his entourage fled Wembley, Alan walked in defeat to his corner, unscathed from the bottles and chaos. He stood shrouded in a blood-soaked towel, facing the reality that he had just lost his title. He was treated by a ringside doctor, largely ignoring the violence unfolding around him. He exited the ring and hoisted his glove in the air. The crowd cheered.

Mick Minter blames the chaos on Leicester football fans, many of whom were there to watch Alan as well as Tony Sibson, another fighter from Leicester who fought on the undercard. Leicester City Football Club, one of England's most popular soccer teams, beat rival Tottenham Hotspur 2-1 at Wembley Stadium that afternoon. It was a long day of drinking for many at the fight.

"All the Leicester football supporters after the football game came over to watch Tony Sibson and Alan Minter fight for the world title," Mick Minter said. "It was them that caused the trouble. It was the football hooligans."

Mick Minter was sitting ringside with his parents when the chaos erupted. He took a bottle off the head.

"It was madness," he said. "I felt sorry for Hagler. It took his glory away."

The Minters hustled back to Alan's dressing room. Chaos continued inside the arena and escalated out on the streets.

"We were all in shock really," Mick Minter said. "Alan was in shock. He commented that Hagler was powerful and that he had done his best."

The Minters composed themselves in the safety of the locker room, as Alan absorbed the loss and doctors tended to his wounds. His cuts required fifteen stitches. He later underwent plastic surgery to repair the deep facial wounds.

Meanwhile, Marvin was rushed into a secure dressing area where he was met by Howard Cosell. The announcer had previously refused to call Marvin by his nickname, Marvelous. Approaching Cosell in the locker room, Marvin looked at him and said, "Let's go with Marvelous tonight."

In the post-fight interview, Marvin was calm and composed, despite the mayhem he had just escaped. He was all-business as he reveled in his victory.

"I was the best I've ever been tonight," he said. "I wanted to put him out cold. That's what I wanted. I thank god the referee stopped the fight because the man couldn't see and I was taking advantage of that."

He added: "This fight will go down as one of the greatest fights in middleweight history."

Rioting, fires, and chaos raged outside the arena. Cops bashed rioters with billy clubs as hooligans smashed windows and threw trash barrels.

Cosell's limo was flipped over. Bertha, Marvin, Ida Mae, Robbie, Goody, and Pat piled into an awaiting car. The vehicle's windshield was smashed.

"Fucking drive man!" Pat yelled.

The mob started rocking their limo. Some shouted: "They robbed him!"

"It was very scary," Bertha said. "They started shaking the car. We were just trying to get out of there. We were just trying to get our behinds in the car and get back to our hotel."

The vehicle was escorted by police from the arena and back toward the Bailey Hotel. The new champion, his family, and team piled out of the limo and scurried into the hotel under heavy police cover. Once safely inside, they were finally free to celebrate at the hotel bar, albeit with an air of solemnity, given the violence that had just unfolded.

Robbie and sparring partner Danny Snyder unfurled an American flag and the group broke into an impromptu rendition of "God Bless America." Wainwright poured tequila and made good on a bet with Bertha to allow her to shave his head if Marvin won the title. Bertha took the straight-edge razor to the attorney's head right there in the hotel bar. It was a new look for Wainwright and one that he would keep for the rest of his life.

Marvin smoked a fat cigar with Goody and Pat and hugged Bertha and Ida Mae. The violence around Wembley died down as Marvin and his entourage partied into the early morning. They went to Heathrow airport the next morning and flew home.

"We're never coming back to this place again," Pat said to Marvin.

Marvin never fought in England again.

"The whole thing was shameful. The whole thing was a travesty. And it was unjust for Marvin," Tris Dixon said. "Because he had finally done it and it was such a big moment for him, and yet he couldn't have that moment. It was taken away from him by that unruly crowd."

While the term "viral" did not yet exist, photos of Marvin being shielded by Goody and Pat, Marvin's name emblazoned on their backs, went global via newswires. Instead of being focused on Marvelous Marvin Hagler finally winning the world middleweight title, the next day's newspaper headlines were about the riot. It was one of those historic sports moments captured in a single, powerful image.

"It's one of the great stains on British boxing," Dixon said.

The UK papers did their thing. The *Western Daily Press* in Bristol splashed "A NATIONAL DISGRACE" across its front page. Scotland's *Daily*

Record's headline screamed "NIGHT OF SHAME." The *Manchester Evening News* wrote: "A NATION OF BAD SPORTS."

Officials launched an inquiry into the riot that led to drinking hours being cut at sporting events and bottles being banned at Wembley, and eventually all British sporting venues.

Inquiries into National Front thuggery in the sport were launched. One Black fighter, Roy Gumbs, told the British Boxing Board of Control that he feared for his life during a fight at London's Alexander Pavilion against white middleweight Mark Kaylor, a Coventry fighter supported by the NF. Gumbs told investigators he feared what would happen if he won.

Kaylor and the NF again drew controversy in 1985 when he and Errol Christie, a Black fighter from Leicester, got into a street fight outside a casino before their scheduled match. The run-up to the fight was filled with threats of NF-led violence, prompting boxing officials and police to impose extra security measures.

Back in Brockton a few days after the fight Marvin was celebrated in one of the biggest parades in the city's history, evoking images of Rocky Marciano in the fifties. Marvin was driven down Main Street in a convertible sedan draped with American flags and a "Marvelous Marvin Hagler" banner. Wearing a tracksuit and his trademark dark sunglasses, Marvin shook hands with kids, smiled and waved as thousands lined the streets.

It had been nearly thirty years since Rocky was celebrated in downtown Brockton. The city had renewed pride. People were excited that a new fighter represented the city. At the end of the route, Marvin stopped and spoke to the press.

"I've fought everybody—the speedballs, the sluggers, the runners, the short guys, the stocky guys," he said. "Lots of times you get up in the morning and feel like crying. You do your running in the park and you keep thinking, 'Damn, this has got to pay off.'"

"For so long, no one knew my name," he added.

EPILOGUE

Marvin left England without his WBC and WBA championship belts. They arrived two weeks later from London and were formally presented to him on October 14, 1980, in Brockton, by Jersey Joe Walcott, who lost his title to Rocky Marciano in Philadelphia in 1952. Having Walcott there in Brockton honoring Marvin brought the two fighters' paths full circle.

Rocky and Marvin were different fighters and different people, but they are inextricably connected. Both loved the Petronelli brothers. Both fought like underdogs. And both are inspirational legends in their hometown.

Marvin went on to defend his title twelve times over seven years. He faced Vito Antuofermo again in 1981 at Boston Garden and beat up the Italian in a gory match that sent Antuofermo to Mass General to get fifty stitches. Antuofermo fought five more times after the bout, going 4-1, before he retired in 1985. He became a character actor and appeared in *Goodfellas*, *The Godfather III*, and *The Sopranos*.

Marvin became a superstar after his thrilling knockout of Thomas Hearns in 1985, and a household name. He appeared in television ads, had endorsement deals, appeared on the cover of *Sports Illustrated*, and was a guest on late-night TV shows, including *Late Night with David Letterman*.

He fought in some of the biggest fights of the era and was a big part of the early success of HBO Boxing and pay-per-view.

In 1983, Marvin defended his title against Roberto Duran, winning a unanimous fifteen-round decision in Vegas. Two years later, he defended his crown against Thomas Hearns in a three-round fight for the ages that many consider one of the greatest ever.

In 1987, he fought Sugar Ray Leonard in his final bout. Everyone in New England knows who won.

In 1991, Marvin returned to London for his brother Robbie Sims's fight at York Hall against Nigel Benn. Alan was ringside and the two fighters met in person for the first time since their 1980 title bout. They spoke briefly ringside and were photographed together in the ring before the fight, which Benn won by KO in the seventh round. Marvin, in a black tuxedo, was cheered by the crowd when he was announced.

Afterward, he addressed the riot that marred his title victory.

"A lot of people have apologized to me, but that is all in the past," he said. "I realize it was only very few people involved and they made the whole country look bad."

He and the Petronelli brothers stayed together until Marvin's retirement in 1987, loyal to each other to the end.

Marvin was inducted into the International Boxing Hall of Fame in 1993.

Goody and Pat trained several other top contenders, including Marvin's brother Robbie Sims, who beat Roberto Duran in 1986; two-time middleweight champion "Irish" Steve Collins; and heavyweight Kevin McBride, who ended Mike Tyson's career via TKO in 2006.

The Petronelli brothers and Marvin remained close for years after Marvin's retirement. He moved to Italy but visited the brothers regularly in Massachusetts and often invited them up to his home in a ski town in New

Hampshire's White Mountains. Marvin and Bertha divorced in 1990. He married his second wife, Kay, in Italy in 2000.

Pat Petronelli died September 2, 2011, at age eighty-nine. Goody's wife of seventy years, Marian, died a month later. Goody died just three months later, on January 12, 2012, of natural causes at his home in Sagamore Beach, Massachusetts, on Cape Cod. He was eighty-eight.

After losing his title, Alan fought only three more times, losing two. He retired just a year after the Wembley bout. He spent his retirement back in Crawley, England, where he owned a pub. He occasionally provided boxing commentary for the BBC and struggled with alcoholism. He died of cancer in September 2020 at age sixty-nine.

In 2014, he was asked about the Hagler fight and expressed regrets.

"I did say that 'Black man' comment but it wasn't meant. I was told to say it," he said. "It was a ridiculous comment . . . I know I shouldn't have said it."

Hagler made no public comments after Alan's death.

Marvelous Marvin Hagler died on March 13, 2021, at his home in the White Mountains of New Hampshire. The official cause of death is "natural causes." He was sixty-six.

In 2024, the city of Brockton unveiled a bronze statue of Marvin placed right next to the former Petronelli Gym building, which was converted to luxury apartments in 2023. It sits in a new park dedicated in his honor. The park includes a tree planted for his mother, Ida Mae, and is located just steps from Main Street on a new street—Marvelous Marvin Hagler Way.

AFTERWORD

I was born and raised in Brockton and grew up with the legends of Rocky Marciano and Marvelous Marvin Hagler. Almost everyone I knew had some connection to one or both fighters. My late father, Roger Wedge, was once Rocky's paperboy. My father also knew the Petronellis and traveled to several of Marvin's fights in New England, Las Vegas, and Atlantic City.

My dad took me to Marvin's second fight against Vito Antuofermo at Boston Garden in 1981 when I was just ten years old. The image of the smoky Garden and Vito, with blood pouring down his face, is one I'll never forget. It ignited my lifelong love of boxing, but, more important, it solidified my personal connection to Marvin. He was just like me—a proud Brocktonian—and I watched with pride as he beat everyone and became one of boxing's greatest fighters.

After a twenty-five-year career in journalism and writing several nonfiction, investigative books, it was a natural next step for me to write about Marvin—and specifically his early life in Newark and the Minter fight.

Starting in 2022, I worked closely with Brockton Mayor Robert Sullivan and his chief-of-staff Sydne Marrow, as well as Marvin's mother, Ida Mae Lang, his friend John Merian, and boxing promoter Peter Czymbor, to produce a bronze statue honoring Marvelous Marvin Hagler. I was honored to be part of the team that made the statue a reality. Thanks to funding secured by Brockton state Representative Gerry Cassidy, fans from across the globe can now visit downtown Brockton and pay their respects to arguably the greatest middleweight who ever lived. Schoolchildren in Brockton can now see and touch a life-sized statue of a hero who grew up in the same neighborhoods as they did. I hope generations of kids go see the statue, take the time to learn about Marvin's incredible journey, and draw inspiration from him.

The day we dedicated the statue in 2024 was a beautiful celebration with Marvin's friends and family, journalists who covered Marvin's career, and fans. Vito Antuofermo attended and recalled spending time in Italy with Marvin in 1990 when both were there filming movies. They became friends after retirement and he said Marvin became "like a brother" to him in their later years.

I told Vito that day that I was at the fight at Boston Garden. It was a short conversation. He clearly did not like to talk about that night.

Marvin did that to a lot of guys.

ACKNOWLEDGMENTS

There are so many people to thank for their assistance in helping make this book possible, but especially Brockton Police Officer Mike Cessarini, who floated the idea of a Hagler book to me a few years ago. I would also, in no particular order, like to thank fight promoter Peter Czymbor, Steve "Sandman" Dunn, Jay Sergio, Brockton Mayor Robert F. Sullivan, Sydne Marrow, Fauzi Hamsho, Mustafa Hamsho, Keith Davidson, ESPN boxing and football host Joe Tessitore, Artie Dias, John Merian, *Boston Globe* writer Emily Sweeney, Tariq Ali, Bryan Roberts for providing me writing space on Cape Cod, Todd duBoef and the team at Top Rank Boxing, my longtime writing partner and friend Casey Sherman, who came up with the title for this book, and my publisher, Kyle Sarofeen, at Hamilcar Publications.

As always, I'm deeply grateful for the love and support from my beautiful wife, Jessica, and our kids, Danielle and Jackson. I love you all so much. All three of you inspire me to be my best every day.

INTERVIEWS

The following people were interviewed for this book between 2023 and 2024:

Mike Culbert, pro boxer
John Merian, Brockton businessman, friend of Marvin
George Krieger, former VP of HBO Sports
George Carney, Brockton businessman
Peter Marciano, brother of Rocky Marciano
Tony Petronelli, pro boxer
J Russell Peltz, boxing promoter
Al Valenti, grandson of promoter Rip Valenti
Mustafa Hamsho, pro boxer
Don Stradley, boxing writer
Mick Minter, Alan Minter's brother
Elizabeth Minter, widow of Alan Minter
Tris Dixon, boxing writer
Artie Dias, Hagler family friend
Cheryl Sims, Marvin's sister
Veronica Hagler, Marvin's sister
Bertha Hagler, Marvin's ex-wife
Jay Sergio, son of Gigi Sergio
Colin Hart, UK boxing journalist
Charles Wigfall, brother of Dornell Wigfall

Leigh Montville, *Boston Globe* journalist
Bob Arum, promoter
Jim Fenton, *Brockton Enterprise* reporter
Richie LaMontagne, pro boxer
Jack Cashin, amateur boxer from Brockton
Stephen Joyce, friend of the Petronelli and Hagler families
Lou DiBella, boxing promoter
Thomas P. O'Neill III, son of former US House Speaker Thomas P. "Tip" O'Neill
Pooch Hall, actor, former amateur boxer from Brockton
Peter Czymbor, boxing promoter
Carlos Acevedo, boxing writer
Frank Lotierzo, boxing writer/analyst
John Curran, Boston boxing trainer

SOURCES

BOOKS

Callis, Tracy, Chuck Hasson, and Mike DeLisa. *Philadelphia's Boxing Heritage: 1876–1976*. Charleston, SC: Arcadia, 2002.

Hughes, Brian, and Damian. *Marvelous: The Marvin Hagler Story*. Sussex, UK: Pitch Publishing, 2016.

Kimball, George. *The Four Kings: Leonard, Hagler, Hearns, Duran, and the Last Great Era of Boxing*. Ithaca, NY: McBooks Press, 2009.

Lee, Sandra S. *Italian Americans of Newark*. Mount Pleasant, SC: Arcadia, 2008.

Lloyd, Melanie. *Sweet Fighting Man: Inside Stories from British Boxers*. York, UK: SportsBooks, 2002.

Stradley, Don. *The War: Hagler–Hearns and Three Rounds for the Ages*. Boston: Hamilcar, 2002.

Watts, Bobby. *Champion Without a Crown: The Man Who Would Be King*. Self-published eBook, 2007.

MAGAZINES
Boxing News
Sports Illustrated
The Ring

NEWSPAPERS
Augusta Chronicle (Augusta, GA)
Associated Press
Baltimore Sun
Birmingham Post (UK)
Boston Globe
Boston Herald
Central New Jersey Home News (New Brunswick, NJ)
Chicago Tribune

Cleveland Plain Dealer
Courier-Post
   (Cherry Hill, NJ)
Coventry Evening
   Telegraph (UK)
Daily Mirror (UK)
Daily Star (UK)
Democrat and Chronicle
   (Rochester, NY)
The Desert Sun (Palm
   Springs, CA)
The Enterprise
   (Brockton, MA)
Evening Chronicle (UK)
Evening Standard (UK)
Evening Telegraph (UK)
Fall River Herald News
   (Fall River, MA)
Fort Lauderdale News
The Guardian

Hull Daily Mail (UK)
Jewish Telegraphic
   Agency
   (New York, NY)
The Journal Times
   (Racine, WI)
Leicester Mercury (UK)
Los Angeles Times
Marion Star
   (Marion, OH)
Miami Herald
Miami News
Milwaukee Sentinel
New York Times
News Tribune
   (Tacoma, WA)
The Observer (UK)
Patriot Ledger
   (Quincy, MA)
Philadelphia Daily News

Philadelphia Inquirer
The Record
   (Hackensack, NJ)
Reuters
Salisbury Post
   (Salisbury, NC)
South Florida
   Sun Sentinel
   (Fort Lauderdale, FL)
Stockton Evening
   and Sunday
   Record
   (Stockton, CA)
Sunday Mirror (UK)
Sunday Oregonian
   (Portland, OR)
Sunday Times (UK)
Times-Tribune
   (Scranton, PA)
Washington Post

WEBSITES

baystatebanner.com
crimemagazine.com
espn.com
fightcity.com

hannibalboxing.com
iberkshires.com
maxboxing.com
nj.com

njspotlightnews.org
olympedia.org
ringtv.com
wbsm.com

ABOUT THE AUTHOR

Dave Wedge is a *New York Times* bestselling author who was an award-winning investigative journalist for the *Boston Herald* for fourteen years. His book about the 2013 Boston Marathon attacks, *Boston Strong: A City's Triumph Over Tragedy*, was adapted for the 2017 movie *Patriots Day*. He has written bestsellers about Tom Brady and "Deflategate," Whitey Bulger and John Lennon. His 2022 book *Riding with Evil: Taking Down the Notorious Pagans Motorcycle Gang* is in development as a feature film.

Blood & Hate is set in 10-point Sabon, which was designed by the German-born typographer and designer Jan Tschichold (1902–1974) in the period 1964–1967. It was released jointly by the Linotype, Monotype, and Stempel type foundries in 1967. Copyeditor for this project was Boutros Salah. The book was designed by Brad Norr Design, Minneapolis, Minnesota, and typeset by Westchester Publishing Services. Printed and manufactured by Lightning Source on acid-free paper.